ON THE
BONE

An unsafe casserole of comic book offal

Featuring mechanically recovered meat
from Viz magazines issues 76 to 81.

**Written and illustrated by
Chris Donald, Simon Donald, Graham Dury,
Simon Thorp and Davey Jones.**

With contributions by
John Fardell and Simon Ecob.
Photography by Colin Davison.
Production Editor Sheila Thompson.
Production Assistant Alex Collier.

Edited by Chris Donald

ISBN 1 902 212 010

Published in Great Britain by John Brown Publishing Limited
The New Boathouse, 136-142 Bramley Road, London W10 6SR.

First printing September 1998.

Printed and bound in the UK, we *think*. But Sheila's
gone home right now so I don't know for sure.

LUVVIE DARLING

VODEON

TONIGHT
KENNETH BRANAGH
IN
KENNETH BRANAGH'S
MERCHANT OF
VENICE
ADAPTED BY
KENNETH BRANAGH
FROM THE ORIGINAL BY
WILLIAM SHAKESPEARE
STARRING KEN, EM,
AND ALL THEIR MATES
ROYAL PREMIERE

OH - I'M SO EXCITED. MY LUVVIE...UP THERE ON THE SILVER SCREEN... YOU'VE FINALLY GOT YOUR REWARD.

TISH AND PISH MY DEAR.

TO FOLLOW MY MUSE AND PLY MY TRADE IS REWARD ENOUGH.

OOH LOOK... HUSH! IT'S STARTING!

DON'T WORRY. IT'LL BE THOSE AWFUL ADVERTS FIRST.

PA-PAA! PA-PAA! PA-PAA! PA-PAA! PA-PAH-PA-PAAA! PAAAOW!

PEARL & DEAN

NOW ON SALE IN THE FOYER... ≷CRACKLE≷ GRAPPLERS HOT DOGS. MMMMM! THEY'RE DELICIOUS! ≷CRACKLE≷...≷POP≷

WELL??

≷CRACKLE≷ FOR A TRUE TASTE OF THE INDIAN CONTINENT...≷CRACKLE≷...THE BENGAL TIGER... FULL ENGLISH MENU AVAILABLE... JUST TWO MINUTES FROM THIS THEATRE... ♫TWANG♫ TWANG ♫...≷CRACKLE≷...≷POP≷

WELL? WHAT DID YOU THINK?

OH, ERM...

BE BRUTAL, BE BRUTAL! BECAUSE MY GOD, THEY WILL BE.

WELL....AH. HOLD ON - THE FILM'S STARTING.

NEXT MORNING...

PHILISTINES! THOSE PHILISTINES! BASTARDS! NOT A SINGLE BLOODY WORD!

OH, KENNY BRANAGH THIS, EMMYPOO THOMPSON THAT, BUT WHAT ABOUT ME?? I SHONE LIKE A STAR WITH THAT HOT DOG... AND NOT A SINGLE BLOODY MENTION IN THE BROADSHEETS!

WELL THAT'S IT. NEVER AGAIN WILL I BE SEDUCED BY THE GAUDY TINSEL OF THE SILVER SCREEN. I SHALL RETURN TO THE BOSOM OF MY FIRST LOVE...

...THE STAGE!

YES. I'LL TREAD THE BOARDS IN THE SUBLIME FOOTSTEPS OF THESPOS. I SHALL GIVE SUCH PERFORMANCES AS LIVE IN THE HEART - FOREVER!

MY AGENT WILL BE PLEASED.

LOUIS? HELLO - IT'S ME...

...LUVVIE...

LUVVIE DARLING.

...DARLING. LUVVIE DARLING.

L-U-V-V-I-E...

LOUIS THEATRICAL AGENCY

AH - HELLO LUVVIE. YES. YOUR CHEQUE FOR THE SAUSAGE ADS IN THE POST...

...LESS MY LITTLE 80% OF COURSE.

WHAT'S THAT? YOU WANT TO DO SOME THEATRE...WELL YOU KNOW I MIGHT JUST HAVE THE PART FOR YOU ALREADY.

HERE WE ARE. IT'S A PLAY ABOUT SOCIAL DEPRIVATION...IT'S ALL ABOUT ONE GIRL'S ATTEMPT TO GET OUT OF THE POVERTY TRAP.

...YEH. IT'S A SORT OF COSTUME DRAMA - YET TOPICAL - WITH A SUBTLE SUBTEXT OF SIBLING RIVALRY.

THE Stage

... BIG CAST, BIG NAMES, MUSICAL PRODUCTION NUMBERS...

WHAT'S THAT LUVVIE? ...NO YOURS ISN'T REALLY A SINGING PART. BUT YOU CAN DANCE A BIT, CAN'T YOU.

Y'KNOW. A BIT OF HOOFING...

IT'S THE FRONT END OF A PANTOMIME COW AGAIN, ISN'T IT.

NO, LUVVIE, NO.

LUVVIE - HOW LONG HAVE I BEEN YOUR AGENT? I AM HURT THAT YOU COULD FOR ONE MOMENT THINK THAT I WOULD OFFER YOU THE FRONT END OF A PANTOMIME COW.

GEOFFREY OUT OF RAINBOW - THE ARSE. YOU'RE THE ARSE END. IT'S AN ACTING CHALLENGE, LUVVIE. IT'S GOT COMEDY UDDERS AND EVERYTHING.

ALRIGHT ALREADY. LISTEN. I'VE JUST HAD A PRODUCER ON THE BLOWER. HE WAS AT THE PREMIERE LAST NIGHT AND HE LIKED WHAT HE SAW.

HE WAS WONDERING IF YOU FANCIED HAVING A PART IN A FILM HE'S MAKING.

...IT'S A LOW BUDGET PRODUCTION... ERM... SORT OF ART HOUSE...

...PROBABLY FOR THE EAST GERMAN MARKET.

AH, YES. AN ARTISTICALLY STARVED POPULATION - HUNGRY FOR CULTURE - NOW THE WALL HAS COME DOWN.

I WOULD BE A CHURL TO DENY THEM THE OPPORTUNITY TO MARVEL AT MY LUMINOUS CINEMATIC PRESENCE.

SO...

SCENE 6... TAKE 42... ACTION!

SCENE 6 TAKE 42
PROD. POP SHOT BITCH
DIR. BILL SHIPTON

AND...CUE LUVVIE!

TAKE THIS YOU HORNY BITCH. YOU LOVE IT WHEN I...ERM... ERM...

OH BUGGER... ≷PROMPT≷

FUCK YOU UP THE ASS!

GODDAMMIT! YOU LOVE IT WHEN I FUCK YOU UP THE ASS!

URGH URGH URGH

FLUFFER ON THE SET PLEASE. HE'S LOSING WOOD.

4

ROGER IRRELEVANT

WE'D BE GLAD TO HELP OUT WITH YOUR CHARITY FUND-RAISING FASHION SHOW, VICAR, AT LEAST IT'S A VARIATION ON THE USUAL VICARAGE FETE THEME

SPLENDID, MRS IRRELEVANT. IT'S TAKING PLACE TODAY IN SLOCOMBES DEPARTMENT STORE, AND ALL PROCEEDS GO TOWARDS A NEW CHURCH ROOF OR A SPARE STEEPLE OR SOME SHIT LIKE THAT

THAT'S ODD! I'M SURE I LEFT MY BICYCLE OUT HERE

SAY YORE PRAYERS, BLACK HAND LUKE, YORE A'GOIN' TER MEET YORE MAKER!

RIGHT BOYS, STRING THE VARMIT UP

ROGER! STOP LYNCHING THE VICAR'S BICYCLE

STAY OUTTA THIS, MA'AM. THIS NO-GOOD COYOTE WAS CAUGHT RUSTLING FONDUE FROM OLD HANK'S CHEESE RANCH. WE DON'T TAKE KINDLY TO FONDUE RUSTLERS IN THESE HERE PARTS

THAT'S ENOUGH! NOW, YOU'RE COMING WITH ME TO HELP THE VICAR WITH HIS CHARITY FASHION SHOW

SHORTLY

SLOCOMBE'S

GRAND CHARITY FASHION SHOW TODAY!

BACKSTAGE

NOW, ROGER, I'D LIKE YOU TO STAND HERE AND DIRECT EACH OF THE MODELS OUT ONTO THE CATWALK, ONE BY ONE

FASHION SHOW

LADIES AND GENTLEMEN, WELCOME TO THE FIRST SLOCOMBES DEPARTMENT STORE CHARITY FASHION SHOW

LATER ON WE'LL BE RAFFLING TOP SUPERMODEL NAOMI MEATBALL'S FAVOURITE TAPEWORM, BUT RIGHT NOW IT'S ON WITH THE FASHION PARADE. AND WE'VE GOT A HOST OF LOVELY LADIES TO MODEL THE VERY LATEST IN CLOTHES DESIGNS

AND FIRST OUT ONTO THE CATWALK IS..... ..ERM..

CRASH!

..AN IRONING BOARD..

WITH SEVERAL SLICES OF BEETROOT RIVETED TO IT'S LEGS

THANKS ROGER, BUT I THINK WE'LL MANAGE THE FASHION SHOW WITHOUT YOUR HELP AFTER ALL

KITCHENWARE

TOYS

LIBBER LIBBER

WHY DON'T YOU HAVE A WANDER AROUND THE REST OF THE STORE?

MEANWHILE

HAVE YOU FINISHED STACKING THAT RATHER PRECARIOUS PYRAMID DISPLAY OF **INCREDIBLY** EXPENSIVE CUT-GLASS CRYSTAL GOBLETS YET?

CUT GLAS

NEARLY. I'VE JUST GOT **ONE MORE** TO PUT ON TOP

CUT GLASS

I JUST HOPE THAT NOTHING **STARTLING OR UNEXPECTED** HAPPENS TO MAKE ME LOSE MY BALANCE AND BRING THE WHOLE DISPLAY CRASHING DOWN, CAUSING THOUSANDS OF POUNDS WORTH OF DAMAGE

YES. IT'S A GOOD JOB WE'RE PUTTING THE DISPLAY UP IN THE MIDDLE OF THE SAHARA DESERT, WHERE THERE'S LITTLE CHANCE OF ANYTHING STARTLING OR UNEXPECTED OCCURRING

CUT GLASS

YES, IT'S JUST AS WELL

THERE. DONE IT.

MEANWHILE BACK IN BRITAIN, AT SLOCOMBES DEPARTMENT STORE

LEATHER

HABERDASHERY

EXCUSE ME YOUNG MAN

COULD YOU DIRECT ME TO THE HAT DEPARTMENT PLEASE?

YES, I ADMIT IT! I ONCE RUBBED A LIZARD AGAINST MICHAEL BUERK'S TONGUE! BUT SO WHAT? WE WERE YOUNG, RECKLESS AND IN LOVE!

AND NOTHING YOU SAY CAN DIMINISH THE MAGIC OF THAT BRIEF, LIZARD-RUBBING MOMENT THAT HAPPENED SO LONG AGO

ROGER! STOP THAT!

G'VEET

WELL REALLY!

PARDON ME, BUT I COULDN'T HELP NOTICING THAT YOUR SON SEEMS TO MAKE NO ATTEMPT WHATSOEVER AT NORMAL HUMAN INTERACTION

ALL HIS RESPONSES ARE TOTALLY IRRATIONAL AND DIVORCED FROM REALITY. IT'S AS IF HE OCCUPIES A COMPLETELY DIFFERENT PLANET

YES, I'M AFRAID YOU'RE RIGHT

EXCELLENT. I'VE GOT THE IDEAL JOB FOR HIM - HE SHOULD FIT IN PERFECTLY

AT THE LOCAL MAGISTRATES COURT

THE NEXT DEFENDANT IS MRS EDITH PEASBODY WHO FAILED TO PAY AN OUTSTANDING COUNCIL TAX CHARGE OF £1.25

SHE IS UNABLE TO PAY THIS BECAUSE HER HOUSE BURNT DOWN AND HER HUSBAND DIED, LEAVING HER A DESTITUTE WIDOW. HAVE THE MAGISTRATES REACHED A DECISION REGARDING THIS CASE?

GUILTY ON ALL COUNTS!

FLIBBET FLIBBET

SPREEEP!

FIFTY YEARS IMPRISONMENT!

TURN HER INTO A LOBSTER!

FINE HER A MILLION POUNDS!

WIBBLE!

MAGISTRATES BENCH

5

If yoU write us Something funny ✪✪✪✪✪✪✪✪✪✪✪✪✪✪✪✪✪✪✪✪✪✪✪✪✪✪✪✪✪✪ we'll turn that bastard into money...

Letterbocks

No Phil Collins required

£50 LETTER

❏ SO Phil Collins is on record as saying he would leave the country if a Labour government ever came to power? Well if I were Tony Blair I would use this promise in Labour's advertising campaign before the next general election. I'm a life long Tory supporter, but I'd vote Labour if it meant that short arsed git would piss off abroad and never come back.

F. CAKE
Bromley

£5 CUSTOMS and Excise tell us that for every pound of drugs they seize ten times that amount gets through. Well if they want fewer drugs getting through why don't they simply seize a smaller amount? Ideally they should seize none at all, since ten times nothing is nothing.

C. PASTY
Padstowe

£5 SO, smug-faced TV hypnotist Paul McKenna can hypnotise boxers and block out pain can he? Then he won't mind giving me a quick demonstration while I clock him round the head with a cricket bat.

T.WATTS
Thurmaston, Leicester

£2.50 I WAS delighted to get a look at C.A Gray's 'Large Fadge' in the last issue. But I can beat that. I often say to my husband "Give us a Bottom Muffin". These saucy snacks are available from a bakers in Beswick.

SHEL TOMLINSON
Cleator Moor, Cumbria

Collins - take your money and stick it up your arse.

Winner makes it all

Winner - fat cunt

❏ IF Michael Winner was an MP he'd have no trouble complying with the Nolan Committee's recommendations concerning declaration of income. In fact, you'd have to prosecute the fat cunt to shut him up and stop him telling every fucker how much loot he's got, where every last penny came from, and what he's been spending it on this week. The fat, arrogant, fat, self-obsessed, draft dodging, fat bastard fat cunt bastard. And his bird's a gold-digging slag heap too. Probably.

A. STENSON
Stockport
(A thin, broke, ex-squaddie Gulf war veteran with no bird, gold-digging slag heaps or otherwise)

Nudes at Ten

❏ IF ONE female news reader started reading the news with her top off everyone would tune in. Before you know it they'd ALL have to get them off in order to compete for viewers. Then all the weather girls would start getting them off too. I can't wait.

JIM CARTER
Oulton, Norfolk

Money for old soap

❏ RECENT issues of Viz have been peppered with cheap defamatory references to your cousins 'Down Under'. You mention our convict heritage, and refer to our lack of intellect. Well if we're so fucking thick how come its YOU who fork out millions to import brainless TV crap like Neighbours?

BRAD PEADON
Sydney, Australia

P.S. Please send me the equivalent of £5 in Australian dollars, and make sure the pen works upside down.

She gets the hump

❏ HOW come when I'm shagging my girlfriend she starts to whine cos I can only last two minutes? You'd think she'd take it as a compliment, the miserable cow.

JOEL YOUNG
Middlesborough

Letterbocks,
P.O. Box 1PT,
Newcastle upon
Tyne, NE99 1PT

£5 AS a loyal citizen of this country I respect the monarchy and have a particular fondness for the Queen Mother. Yet ironically I am looking forward to the day of her demise. Because as a civil servant I will get a day off work when they bury her.

S. G.
Shropshire

Load of old cobblers

❏ I'VE OFTEN heard people say that "Thyme is a great heeler". As a reputable cobbler of some fifty years standing I know for a fact that only prolonged practice in cobbling and heel replacement can make you a great heeler. The chances of a garden herb being able to substitute the solidity of a solid man-made sole are futilistic to say the least.

PAUL GREENWOOD
Wigan

❏ I THINK that Kenneth Clarke deserves at pat on the back. In a day when politicians are clamouring to have affairs with dolly birds and M.P.s are often judged on the looks of their wives, it's nice to see that the Chancellor of the Exchequer thinks enough of his dear old mum to take her along to his budget day speech.

J. DOUGHNUT
Wrigleyspearmint, Gum

Storm of protest

❏ IN THE song 'Yo never walk alone' Ge Marsden advises listen 'When you walk throug storm, hold your head high'. However as light ing always strikes protr ing objects not only is t advice wrong but it is a potentially fatal. Marsden and his gulli fans would do well to n that in stormy condition is best to present as sma surface area as possible the atmosphere a crouch down close to ground in the open aw from large objects such trees.

S. R
Bakersfi

Door catch

£5 IN ISSUE 75 yo correspondent T. Kitch suggests that if Lloy bank wished to genuin help left handed peo they would put hinges a door handles on BOT sides of their doors. would however point that a door handle on o one side of the door equally useful to both ri and left handed people going in you have to one hand, and going the other; furthermo my own experiments ha confirmed that by putti hinges and handles both sides of a door y render it immovable.

DR IAIN R. MCN
Lecturer in Phys
University of Newcas
upon Ty

* Elementary Dr McNab

PRIVATE PARKING FOR GOBBLERS Patrons ONLY

GILLIAN Taylforth should live in America. There they thoughtfully provide special places to park if you fancy giving your boyfriend's bellend a quick peel and polish, as this recent photo (above) proves.

ROY CARTER
Mountsorrel, Leicestershire

Follow that ambulance

I READ with interest S.Roll of Bakersfield's letter regarding lightening and the sixties pop singer Gerry Marsden (Letterbox, this issue). As a solicitor specialising in injuries compensation and negligence claims I would be most interested to hear from anyone who, upon reflection, thinks they may perhaps have suffered some physical injury or had an accident at any time in the past 35 years as a result of listening to songs recorded by Merseyside pop stars of the 60's, no matter how tenuous their case may appear. I offer initial consultations free of charge.

A. CHASER (SNR.)
Chaser, Golddigger & Shark
104 Broad Street, Leeds

READERS wishing to charm their birds kecks off could do a lot worse than buying them item A from page 302 of Freeman's Catalogue. Or item L on page 303. In fact just about anything from pages 301 to 313.

A.W.
Horley, Surrey

IN RESPONSE to your reader who can drink five pints of lager without needing a piss (Letterbocks, issue 75). I regularly drink five pints of piss, and have never needed a lager.

A. SOUTHERN-SOFTY
Lahndan

I WAS hoping you could help me by printing the following message for my husband who popped out for a pint of milk two years ago and hasn't returned. "Barry. If there's no silver top, semi-skimmed will do".

MRS OLIVIA BRITTON
Didsbury, Manchester

TVs on TV

THERE has been a lot of TV coverage recently devoted to the subject of transvestites. I can't help feeling there are enough ugly women in this world already without men having to dress up as them.

JIM MCATEER
London SE15

MOTORISTS. When asking directions from a woman always look for one with small tits as they've usually got more brains. God seldom gives them both.

G. Kiss
Crawley

CARAVAN owners planning to use the A5 between Betwys-y-Coad and Llangollen on the first day of the Easter bank holiday (5th April), please stay at home. I'm visiting my girlfriend that day and I really can't afford to be seven hours late.

P. Bandwagon
Clwyd

CAREER women. Save time getting ready for work in the mornings by putting on five pairs of knickers on Monday. Then each morning simply whip off the top pair and hey presto! There's a clean pair underneath.

S. Stain
London

P.S. Come Friday drop a toilet freshener down your pants to reduce the smell of halibut.

GERMAN sex perverts. Rig up a four foot length of garden hose with a shower head on the end, drink ten pints of lager then attach the other end to your knob. Hey presto! Your own personalised golden shower!

A. Bain
Manchester

TOP TIPS

A BICYCLE pump used backwards makes a handy makeshift vacuum cleaner.

T. Elm
Hornchurch, Essex

COLLECT your farts in sandwich bags during the winter. Store them in a safe place, and come the summer these handy "Pump packets" will make ideal firelighters for barbecues, etc.

Andy Rogers
Fenham

MAKE your arse into an 'Anus fly trap' by wedging it open with a matchstick attached to a length of string. When a fly lands on your chocolate starfish yank the string and SNAP! Got the bastard.

Sid
Macclesfield

PROBLEMS storing your CDs? Hang cotton threads from the ceiling and close your CD cases around them to produce your very own walk-through CD library. It also doubles as an interesting mobile for young children.

Greig Harper
Peterlee, Co. Durham

A BALL of Edam cheese with the centre carefully removed makes an ideal crash helmet for mountain bikers.

J. Ouster
Port Erin, Isle of Man

PREVENT your ears from being bitten off in the pub by Sellotaping them flat to the side of your head.

P. Ash
Kent

NEXT time you have a large family gathering such as a wedding or birthday party don't invite Angela Lansbury. If she does turn up, call the police, an ambulance and the coroner immediately.

S. Hammer
Bromsgrove

STAR Trek captains. When your ship is in imminent danger of being destroyed, save a great deal of hassle by thinking of the last thing you could possibly try, which might just work, and do that first.

J. L. Pickard
Space

A STIFF toothbrush makes an ideal comb for trendy sideburns.

Spencer D. Group
Irby, Wirral

LEFT over Christmas tree 'needle drop' spray can be used on pets to prevent them dropping hairs on the carpet.

P. Cherry
Avon

The SIMON SALAD-CREAM Story — Part Eight — A NEW ARRIVAL AT RADIO 1

Continued on page 16

The MAN in the PUB

Britain's most ill-informed columnist.

Guess who's got AIDS

☐ GUESS who's got AIDS. Go on then, 'ave a guess. Alright, I'll tell ya. *Prince Andrew*, that's who. Yeah! It's true. This posh bloke told a mate of mine. God's honest truth. They're coverin' it up. Gonna say it was a kidney infection when he pegs it. Or leukemia. Just you wait an' see.

☐ YOU KNOW that Patsy Kensit's ditched her fella, don'tcha. That bloke out of Simple Minds. But do you know why? *It's great this is.* Mate o'mine in the music business told me. Guess what? **He wears a nappy!** Yeah, great big nappy. That's why he keeps loosin' his birds. It's true. Can't control the old waterworks, apparently. Mind you, that Patsy Kensit, eh? *Phoooaaar! I would*, I can tell ya. *Cor!* Not 'alf.

Same size heads

● Did you know that your head never grows? Ever. Stays exactly the same size all through your life. Think about it. You look at any baby's head, right. Exactly the same size as yours or mine.

☐ THIS mate o'mine's got a garage, right. Guess who comes in the other day tryin' to sell him knocked off car radios. Only *Gazza*, the footballer. Yeah! What a bloody nerve. *Fifty grand a week* he gets for kickin' a ball about, and he still goes out nicking car radios.

Dungeon under house

☐ I'll tell you what. You know that little baldy Labour bloke, Gerald Kauffman, the MP? He's got a *dungeon* under his house, he has. *Yeah!* A fuckin' dungeon. They reckon he tortures people in it, an' then he kills 'em. Probably eats 'em an' all. Wouldn't surprise me. Mate o'mine's into bondage an' all that. Says that's *definite*.

That bloke Kauffman

☐ Amanda Donoghue, right? Actress? Fridge full o'spunk. No, straight up! She keeps it all in them little plastic film canisters. Got a fridge full of the bleedin' stuff. God knows what she does with it though. Bloody screw loose there if you ask me, mate.

Apollo nonsense was bollocks

YOU KNOW all that Apollo rocket nonsense? Bollocks that was. They made it all up. Never went to the Moon. Filmed it in a studio somewhere in America. In the desert it was. It's all shot in slow motion. Apparently, the bit where they land, *if you look close enough you can see a telegraph pole in the background.* Clear as day. Mind, I shouldn't really be tellin' you this. They shot the cameraman afterwards. Made it look like an accident. Knew too much, y'see.

One of them space rockets

Pigs CAN'T swim

☐ YOU EVER seen a pig swim, eh? Think about it. No mate, you 'aven't. Know why? They **can** swim, right, but they **can't,** you see. Cos if they **did** swim they'd cut their throats. Straight up! It's the shape o'their trotters. If they swam they'd cut themselves to ribbons an' bleed to death. *And you know what?* An English pig can't shag an Australian pig. Impossible. Cos their cocks and their fannies, right, go round and round y'see. Twirly, like. And pigs from the *north* of the world, their's go round one way, and pigs from the *south* go round the other way. Like *clockwork* an' *anti-clockwork*, you know. It's true that. You ask a farmer.

This bird had no knickers on

■ I was in 'ere the other night, right, an' this bird walks in... *fuck me!* She was *gorgeous!* An' I'll tell you what. She had no knickers on. You could tell by the way she was standin'. Givin' me the eye all night she was. *Phooarr!* Anyway, whose round is it?

DADDY, CAN I GO AND PLAY ON THE BEECH?

Spoilt Bastard

11

Ghosts 'not scary anymore'

*By our ghostwriter
PHIL SPECTRE
and his Wall of Sound*

GHOSTS are no longer as scary as they used to be, according to a new report set to be published a fortnight next Wednesday teatime.

The spooky survey was commissioned by the Association of Ghost Train Operators to try and explain a dramatic drop in passenger revenue in recent years. However it could have far wider implications. For experts fear that by the year 2025 children will no longer be scared of ghosts at all.

Monsters

The scariness of ghosts has suffered in the face of fierce competition from two main rivals, monsters and space aliens. In their heyday ghosts were by far the scariest thing in Britain, with 98% of children under the age of twelve and one in five adults scared of them. But the sixties sci-fi explosion and the advent of TV have caused a tidal wave of competition, and a succession of scary things - from monsters to Martians, and from Dracula to dinosaurs - have started to give kids the creeps.

Creeps

Len Murray, secretary of the official ghosts union the National Association for the Dead and Departed, lays the blame for the present problem squarely at the feet of space aliens. "It all began in the sixties with the Daleks, and now it has simply got out of hand. Ghosts can't compete. There must be controls put in place to protect the interests of our members", he said.

Nerds

Like aliens, monsters too have had a field day frightening children in recent years. And dinosaurs are the latest in a long line of horrible creatures to capture the imagination of children, and make them hide under their bedclothes. But Mr Murray fears that bringing dinosaurs to life in the film

Jurassic Park was irresponsible and could lead to a 'double whammy' effect. "How long is it going to be before children start having nightmares about the ghosts of

dead dinosaurs?" he asked. "Things are spiralling out of control, and unless the Government act soon it is only a matter of time before youngsters are faced with the terrifying prospect of the ultimate scary thing - the ghost of a dead alien space monster", warned Mr Murray.

What shits up the stars?

We asked a few famous faces what frightens them most of all. Former Russian gymnast Olga Korbut, now a Barbados taxi driver, told us that ghosts were the last things on her mind when she won the Olympic Games a long time ago. "As a child I was always scared of crocodiles", she confessed. "I could never bring myself to watch Peter Pan, and I still hide hide under my bedclothes when I hear my alarm clock ticking", she told us.

Crocodile's give Korbut (balancing on parallel bar, above) the creeps, while Frankenstiens give Martin Chivers the shivers. Meanwhile Peter Cushion (below) is Hammer horrified... of cars!

Sex Cases

Former England and Spurs centre forward Martin Chivers wasn't afraid of a hard tackle in his heyday. Now living in Denmark where he runs a successful ecclesiastical supplies business, he confessed to having one secret fear. "I must admit - I've always been scared of Frankensteins", he told us. "I don't know if its the bolts in their necks, or their clumpy boots, but even now I shit my pants whenever a Frankenstein comes on the telly".

Hammer horror star **Peter Cushion** showed no sign of fear in over 850,000 film appearances. But in reality Cushion was desperately scared of cars. "In his later years he'd hang around the street all day, appearing to follow people about. Often they would call the police. But all he wanted to do was follow them across the road. He was terrified of cars, and was scared to go near a road by himself", Peter's former neighbour and T.V. Lottery Queen Anthea Turner told us.

Dooby dooble blow!

SAVE OUR SPOOKS!

BOLLOCK brained Brussels bureautwats have sprouted a hair raising scheme that will send shivers up the spine of spirits all over Britain.

The Belgium based buffoons want to see a single European spook replace existing ghosts, poltergeists and apparitions by the year 2000.

Shockwaves

Plans to exorcise our estimated 200,000 spooks - and replace them with a standard EEC Euroghost - have sent shockwaves through haunted houses all over Britain. And last night the plan was attacked by Tory MP Sir Anthony Regents-Park.

Heatwaves

"Of course I don't believe in ghosts, and I'm certainly not scared of them. But even so, this is yet another example of Brussels bureaucracy gone mad".

Eurocrats plan to exorcize the Great British Ghoul

Of all the EEC member states Britain has by far the greatest number of ghouls. However traditional figures such as the Lady in White and Headless Horsemen have lost ground in recent years to more contemporary phenomena. These range from ubiquitous poltergeists throwing kitchen crockery to the equally common strange and unexplained presences in cars (accompanied by a sudden change of temperature) experienced by motorists driving alone late at night near the scene (and on the anniversary of) an horrific road accident.

Hi Tensions

Labour's Terry Nice was last night reluctant to condemn the EEC proposals. "Obviously we need to look very closely at the whole issue of ghosts and whether we believe in them and what, if anything, they should look like, because its an issue that affects all of us, but other than that I'm not going to say anything and I'll just sit on the fence hedging my bets and smiling a lot and hope that everybody will vote for me at the next election".

Internet attacker gets two years

In the first case of its kind in Britain a man has been convicted of assault after robbing a 72 year old pensioner on the computer Internet.

Wayne Pile, an unemployed 18 year old, was sentenced to two years in prison after a jury found him guilty of assault and robbery at the home of Percival Francis, a retired clerk of Putney, South London. Mr Francis had just sat down at his computer and was preparing to write a letter to a relative when Pile, who was 200 miles away in Sheffield, struck.

Tavares's

The robber was apprehended by police after an alert computer operator in Glossop spotted him acting suspiciously outside an E mail address in Hull. Detective Inspector Eric Fletcher who lead the investigation believes that computer crime is on the increase.

"The criminal will not hesitate to explore new avenues of crime, and as technology advances we must ensure that police resources are updated and criminal legislation constantly reviewed in order to remain abreast of the situation". He described the Putney attack as particularly vicious. Mr Francis was knocked to the ground and required hospital treatment for cuts and bruises. Pile escaped through the Internet with less than twenty pounds in cash and a pension book.

The Floaters's

In a similar case an American teenager was fined by a court in Ohio for throwing a waterbomb out of Windows 95 and hitting a passing pedestrian in Hong Kong.

14

SPOT THE CLUE

WITH TV'S CELEBRITY CHEF DELIA SMITH

GREETINGS EAGLE-EYED SLEUTHS EVERYWHERE! I'VE COOKED UP A SIZZLING ADVENTURE THIS WEEK - AND IT'S CALLED **THE AFFAIR OF THE ENLARGED BEES**

SCOTLAND YARD: THE OFFICE OF INSPECTOR SHARPE

SHARPE! A MURDER HAS BEEN COMMITTED AT DR GRIMSDYKE'S BEE-ENLARGEMENT CLINIC

ON MY WAY, CHIEF

SHORTLY

THANK GOODNESS YOU'RE HERE INSPECTOR. I'M DR GRIMSDYKE

BEE-ENLARGEMENT CLINIC
DR J. GRIMSDYKE MD

MY JUNIOR ASSISTANT BEE-ENLARGER HAS BEEN **STABBED TO DEATH!**

I FOUND THE BODY HERE AT NOON - WITH THIS MESSAGE SCRAWLED ON THE WALL NEXT TO HIM

STOP MAKING BEES FATTER OR I'LL KILL AGAIN!

HMM. WHAT EXACTLY IS THE PURPOSE OF YOUR CLINIC, DR GRIMSDYKE?

WE MAKE BEES PLUMPER, INSPECTOR. YOU SEE, I AM CONVINCED THAT BEES ARE **TOO THIN**. THEY ARE SKINNY LITTLE CREATURES WITH GAUNT FACES, AND CHEEKBONES LIKE JEREMY IRONS

BEE WEIGHT

SO I HAVE DEVOTED MY LIFE TO FATTENING UP BEES BY FORCE-FEEDING THEM CAKES, BISCUITS AND SWEETS

IT IS MY DREAM THAT ONE DAY, EVERY BEE IN THE LAND WILL BE **GROSSLY OBESE**

IMAGINE IT, INSPECTOR! SWARMS OF ENORMOUSLY-FAT BEES, ALL BUZZING AROUND WITH GREAT BIG CHUBBY CHEEKS LIKE A HAMSTER!

A NOBLE AMBITION, DR GRIMSDYKE

STOP MAKING BEES FATTER I'LL KILL AGAIN!

BUT SOMEBODY IS PREPARED TO COMMIT MURDER IN ORDER TO PREVENT YOU FROM ACHIEVING IT

HM. LOOKS LIKE THE MURDERER SLIPPED IN THROUGH THIS OPEN WINDOW

DID YOU NOTICE ANY SUSPICIOUS CHARACTERS HANGING ROUND OUTSIDE YOUR CLINIC THIS MORNING?

I DIDN'T, INSPECTOR - BUT MY COOK, MRS DANVERS, MAY HAVE DONE

THE KITCHEN WINDOW OVERLOOKS THE STREET, YOU SEE. MRS DANVERS MAY WELL HAVE GLANCED OUT AND SPOTTED THE MURDERER LURKING OUTSIDE

BUT IN THE KITCHEN

OOH, I'M SORRY, I DIDN'T SEE A THING. I'VE BEEN FAR TOO BUSY COOKING DR GRIMSDYKE'S DINNER TO BE LOOKING OUT OF WINDOWS THIS MORNING!

I ALWAYS TAKE GREAT PRIDE IN MY ROAST BEEF DINNERS, INSPECTOR. THEY'RE MY SPECIALITY, YOU KNOW

LOOKS LIKE WE'VE DRAWN A BLANK, INSPECTOR

I WOULDN'T BE SO SURE!

CAN YOU SPOT THE CLUE?

MRS DANVERS IS LYING, DR GRIMSDYKE - AND I BELIEVE SHE IS THE MURDERER OF YOUR ASSISTANT

FOLLOW ME, AND WE'LL SEE IF MY SUSPICIONS ARE CORRECT

OUTSIDE

AH-HA! JUST AS I THOUGHT!

GREAT SCOTT! WHAT'S THAT THING HOVERING OVER THE ROOF OF MY CLINIC?

IT'S A SECRET MINIATURE SPACE STATION FOR BEES, WITH NUCLEAR MISSILES POINTED AT CHINA

YOUR COOK MRS DANVERS IS EMBARKED ON AN EVIL PLAN TO CONQUER THE WORLD!

YOU'RE A CLEVER MAN, INSPECTOR. YES, MY SECRET MINIATURE SPACE STATION IS ENTIRELY OPERATED BY SPECIALLY TRAINED BEES

AT MY COMMAND, THOSE BEES WOULD HAVE FIRED THE NUCLEAR MISSILES AT CHINA, AND I WOULD HAVE RULED THE WORLD

HOWEVER, DR GRIMSDYKE'S BEE-ENLARGEMENT CLINIC WAS MAKING MY TRAINED BEES **TOO FAT** TO FLY UP TO THE SPACE STATION

UNABLE TO GET THEIR FAT BEE ARSES OFF THE GROUND, THEY JUST SAT AROUND EATING BISCUITS INSTEAD OF NIPPING UP AND FIRING NUCLEAR MISSILES AT CHINA

MRS DANVERS, I ARREST YOU FOR THE MURDER OF DR GRIMSDYKE'S ASSISTANT

AND ALSO FOR POINTING NUCLEAR MISSILES AT CHINA, AND TRYING TO TAKE OVER THE WORLD

NICE WORK INSPECTOR. BUT HOW DID YOU KNOW MRS DANVERS WAS GUILTY? WHAT GAVE HER AWAY?

SIMPLE. MRS DANVERS CLAIMED THAT ROAST BEEF DINNERS WERE HER SPECIALITY - **BUT THIS WAS CLEARLY NOT THE CASE!**

DID YOU SPOT THE CLUE?

IF ROAST BEEF DINNERS HAD **TRULY** BEEN HER SPECIALITY, THEN HER ROAST POTATOES WOULD HAVE BEEN GOLDEN-BROWN WITH CRUNCHY EDGES - YET I NOTICED THAT THEY LOOKED RATHER BLAND AND LACKING IN CRISPINESS

TO HAVE GIVEN HER ROAST POTATOES NICE CRUNCHY EDGES, MRS DANVERS SHOULD HAVE VIGOROUSLY SHAKEN THE POTATOES IN A PAN AFTER BOILING, THEN BASTED THEM WITH HOT FAT AND POPPED THEM INTO THE OVEN (220°C/GAS MARK 7) FOR 40-50 MINUTES. SPRINKLE WITH A LITTLE CRUSHED SALT, AND SERVE.

Continued from page 9

I'm afraid the garden has gone completely wild.

Here, grab hold of these and I'll show you where to start.

I know it's small compared to Lady Chatterley's, but it's got a lot of potential.

I thought you could start by tidying it up a bit... then I'd like you to weed the flower beds and build a rockery over there.

LATER...

Fuckin''ell!! It took me two days to do that garden and I never even got a cuppa, never mind a shag. I could murder a pint

AT THE BAR...

Gosh! You're that hunky heart throb actor Sean Bean aren't you?

Why yes, as a matter of fact I am!

Oh God! I can't believe this!! I'm such a big fan...

...of football. I just love talking about football. You're in the new film about football aren't you? It's great to meet a fellow fan. Sheffield United man, yeah?

Oh gawd!

Good old Blades! Great result against Arsenal. Pity about the league form. What do you think of Howard Kendall? Has he made a difference? Totally different style to Bassett of course. Likes his football does Kendall. Keeps it on the deck eh?

Now... I was never too sure about Tony Currie. Hell of a player in his day... bit like Le Tissier really. But one swallow doesn't win any silverware, Sean. Football's a funny old game...

It's about commitment. You want players who are going to give 110% for the full ninety minutes, 'cos at the end of the day it's players that wins games, not goals. Of course goals help. All the best teams score goals...

EVENTUALLY...

Jesus, what a bore! I can't believe that - it took me two hours to get served!

Excuse me!

Sorry, to interrupt you but...

... my mate over there reckons you're that hunky, heart throb actor out of the new James Bond movie. Are you?

Bean's the name. Sean Bean. Secret Agent 006 at your service.

Perhaps you and your friend would like to join me for a drink? Martini of course - shaken not stirred!

16

DISILLUSIONED WITH LIFE AS A STAR LOOKALIKE PETER STAGGERED BACK TO THE HAIRDRESSERS.

AND HE EMERGED MOMENTS LATER WITH HIS OLD HAIRCUT BACK IN PLACE...

PETER RANG DEBBIE AND ASKED FOR A CHANCE TO APOLOGISE. SHE AGREED TO MEET HIM FOR A DRINK....

The End

CD 1/96 Photography by Colin Davison (this issue and the one before)

R.I.P. (Rest In Paradise)

Rolling Stone gathers swish £250,000 grave

Millionaire Mick will be in Heaven when he moves into his magnificent Montserrat grave. Our artist's impression shows how it might look.

Rock'n'Roll senior citizen Mick Jagger has splashed out a quarter of a million pounds on a luxury grave on the sun drenched Caribbean island of Monserrat.

And millionaire Mick is set to splash out a cool half million more lavishly converting the graveyard gaff into a tomb fit for a king.

Plot

The Monserrat plot, in an exclusive corner of the island's most prestigious cemetery, brings to five the total number of final resting places owned by the Rolling Stone. Jagger, now 72, bought his first grave in 1964, paying just over £2000 for a modest plot in his local cemetery at Richmond in Surrey. Since then he has added a small crypt in the Highlands of Scotland, a lavish $2 million marble tomb in the Belle Air district of Beverly Hills and a small weekend urn on the West Bank in Paris.

Mad about graves - Mick looks forward to being committed - to the Earth!

Keg

This latest addition was an impulse buy made during a tea break in the recording of the Stone's latest album 'Voodoo Lounge'. "Mick was taking a break from recording when he just happened to drive past the cemetery. He saw the grave and just fell in love with it", a Stones insider told us.

Kex

"It wasn't for sale but he made an offer the owner couldn't refuse." The previous occupant was exhumed and moved out that afternoon.

After splashing quarter of a million on the grave itself Jagger will now lay out twice as much again on lavish refurbishments before it is ready for moving in. "Mick has his own very personal tastes", our source told us "and he'll want to get it just right, whatever the cost". Jagger is rumoured to have spent over £80,000 revamping his Richmond grave recently before sacking the grave digger and ordering the work to be carried out again.

Shreddies

Mick has told showbiz pals that after his death he intends to spread his time between his graves, spending a few months of the year in each. "Knowing Mick he'll still get around a bit after he's gone", our source confirmed. "But he's really a home loving man and I think he'll spend most of his time in his Richmond plot near his family and friends."

What a plot he's got! Mick snapped up his favourite final resting place in Richmond (above) for only £2000 in 1964. But he's also planning to push up daisies at the remote Scottish church yard below where he owns a magnificent detatched stone crypt set in 10 yards of grass.

BLAST ROCKS BRIT POP AWARDS

Brit Ekland - left in tears after pop explosion wrecked ceremony.

THE BRIT EKLAND Pop Awards ended in confusion last night after a bottle of home made ginger beer exploded showering tables with broken glass. The ceremony, which was taking place in a function room above the Red Lion pub in Watford, had to be abandoned in the chaos which followed.

Film star Miss Ekland, 58, had been announcing nominations in her annual awards for soft drinks when the bottle burst on a table behind her.

She was clearly shocked by the explosion but bravely attempted to carry on. Shortly afterwards she paused and appeared unsteady on her feet. She was then lead away, clearly in some distress.

The awards were launched by Miss Ekland in 1967 in recognition of her favourite fizzy drinks, and ran for twelve successive years until they were abandoned in 1979 due to lack of media interest. Since then Miss Ekland has lead a vigorous solo campaign for their reinstatement and last night's awards were to have marked their return after an absence of 17 years.

It is not known whether the ceremony will be rearranged. Less than half the invited audience of 23 had attended, and a spokesman for Miss Ekland said the envelope containing winners names had been lost in the mayhem following the explosion. Brit Ekland was last night unavailable for comment.

HOBBY HORSE

DUE TO A CLERICAL ERROR AT THE SPERM BANK, YOUNG NOBBY DOBBS HAD BEEN BORN WITH THE HEAD OF A HORSE.

IT'S THE SCHOOL DISCO TONIGHT READERS, AND I'M *SO* LOOKING FORWARD TO IT. IT'LL BE GREAT FUN

I'M GOING TO ASK CLARE WILLIAMS FOR A DANCE, BECAUSE I FANCY HER. SHE'S GOT A REALLY PRETTY SMILE

BUT SORRY NOBBY, BUT I CAN'T 'ALLOW YOU INTO THE DISCO WITH THAT FREAKISH HORSE'S FACE OF YOURS. YOU WOULD SIMPLY SPOIL THE OTHER KIDS' ENJOYMENT

YOU SEE, EVERYONE IS REPULSED BY YOUR HORSE-LIKE APPEARANCE. NOBODY LIKES YOU, AND THERE'S NOTHING YOU CAN DO ABOUT IT

IF I WERE YOU, SON, I'D JUST RESIGN MYSELF TO A LIFE OF UTTER SOLITUDE, AND NEVER EVER HAVING ANY FRIENDS...

...EVER.

CRIMMINY! A LIFE WITHOUT EVER HAVING ANY FRIENDS!

HOW ON EARTH AM I GOING TO SPEND ALL THOSE ENDLESS DAYS ON MY OWN, WITH NO ONE TO TALK TO?

I KNOW...

I'LL FIND MYSELF A *HOBBY* INSTEAD

STAMP-COLLECTING SOUNDS LIKE A GOOD LAUGH. I'LL GIVE IT A TRY. ›AHEM‹ HERE GOES...

ONE FIRST CLASS STAMP PLEASE

THAT'S TWENTY SIX PEE

SUCCESS! WHAT A MAGNIFICENT START TO MY COLLECTION

HELLO. I'M A FELLOW STAMP COLLECTOR. ISN'T THAT A 1996 TWENTYSIXPENNY ORANGE?

YES!

SNATCH!

RIP SHRED TEAR

THERE. BY DESTROYING YOUR STAMP, I'VE INCREASED THE RARITY VALUE OF MY OWN COLLECTION

THANKS LAD. YOU'VE JUST MADE ME CONSIDERABLY RICHER

PERHAPS *GARDENING* WILL BE A MORE REWARDING HOBBY; WHO KNOWS? I COULD BECOME THE NEXT ALAN TITCHMARSH

EXCEPT WITHOUT BEING QUITE SUCH A TWAT, HOPEFULLY

ONE WEEK LATER

HOW DO YOU LIKE THE MINIATURE JAPANESE 'BONSAI' TREE WHAT I'VE GROWN?

IT WAS *NEIGH* PROBLEM FOR SOMEONE WITH MY 'HORSE-SENSE'

EXCUSE ME. I'M FROM THE MINISTRY OF TRANSPORT

WE'VE JUST DECIDED TO BUILD A ROAD OVER THE TOP OF YOUR TREE

WHUMP!

THERE. THAT SHOULD EASE A BIT OF TRAFFIC CONGESTION

BAH!

I'VE DECIDED TO BE AN AUTOGRAPH HUNTER INSTEAD

NOW I JUST NEED TO FIND SOMEONE FAMOUS WHOM I CAN BECOME FANATICALLY OBSESSED WITH

AHA. THERE'S MRS TIMMS FROM THE CORNER SHOP

SHE'S A LEADING LIGHT IN THE LOCAL AMATEUR DRAMATIC SOCIETY

YES NOBBY, WHAT CAN I GET YOU?

I'D LIKE A SIGNED GLOSSY PHOTO OF YOU PLEASE, MRS TIMMS

I'M GOING TO PIN IT UP ON MY BEDROOM WALL. THEN I'M GOING TO HUNT YOU DOWN AND KILL YOU

TCH. TYPICAL. IT'S WE, THE FANS, WHO MAKE THEM INTO STARS — AND HOW DO THEY REPAY US?

WITH A CLIP ROUND THE EAR, THAT'S HOW!

LATER

I'M GOING TO TEACH MYSELF HOW TO MAKE BALLOON ANIMALS PFFFF

THIS SHOULD STRETCH MY CREATIVE CAPACITIES TO THEIR LIMITS

WHOOPS!

POP

MY BALLOON'S BURST

CRASH

THE NOISE MADE BY YOUR BALLOON POPPING HAS CAUSED MY PASSENGER JET TO FALL TO PIECES, AND PLUMMET TO THE GROUND

WELL YOU CAN BLIMMING WELL JUST STICK THAT AEROPLANE BACK TOGETHER AGAIN

AT LAST I'VE FOUND THE PERFECT HOBBY, READERS. THIS REAL-LIFE GIANT SIZE "AIRFIX MODEL KIT" WILL KEEP ME OCCUPIED FOR AGES

NOW, WHICH WAY UP DO THE WINGS GO AGAIN, MR PILOT?

19

Martin's laugh in

Deadpan Dean is in high spirit's world

Dean - having last laugh

AMERICAN showbiz legend Dean Martin who died on Christmas Day has surprised mortuary staff in California with his amazing sense of humour.

Workers at the swish $10,000 a slab Los Angeles morgue say the brave comic was sitting up and cracking jokes with fellow corpses only minutes after his post mortem examination.

"He had the Coroner in stitches with a succession of quick fire gags", one senior mortician told reporters. "He certainly wasn't allowing his death to get him down".

Heart

Only minutes earlier Martin had been told by doctors that his heart had stopped working, and that

he would be dead forever. "He didn't seem too concerned. He just laughed and asked if we could put three pairs of shoes in his coffin - because soon he'd be going six feet under", one witness revealed afterwards.

Slits

Celebrated boozer Martin later smiled and waved to fans as he was whisked in a coffin from the exclusive Belle Air Chapel of Rest where he had been staying to a local crematorium where his remains were cremated. En route he

told undertakers he was thirsty and jokingly asked whether the hearse could stop at a liquor store.

Fuzzbox

One technician at the $20,000 an oven crematorium later said Martin's ashes were in high spirits, and they had smiled and chatted happily with other remains while waiting to be poured into their swish $500 urn.

Sting Storm!

Sting - 'better helmets'

SINGER Sting sailed into a new storm yesterday when he told a Swedish pop magazine that Britain should have surrendered to Germany in the Second World War.

"I really believe we should have surrendered to Hitler", he told a reporter from Bonken Zpunken magazine. "It would have saved a lot of time and money. A lot of bad stuff has been written about Hitler, but the guy must have had some good points. I don't think he's been given a very good press recently". When he was asked which side he would have chosen to fight on Sting replied "Definitely the Germans. They had better helmets".

Clout

This is the second time in a week that Sting has opened his mouth and put his foot in it. On Monday he was reported to have said that primary school children should be given free heroin and that ginger babies should be drowned in a bucket.

Bangles

These latest untimely remarks are bound to

offend the relatives of servicemen and women who lost their lives during the five year conflict (not to mention members of the Jewish community who suffered so badly at the

hands of Hitler) when they read them in this paper tomorrow.

George hits the jackpot!

A Middlesborough grandad was last night celebrating with family and friends after finding a straight piece of wood in his local B&Q home improvements store.

George Clayton, a retired scaffolder and keen DIY enthusiast popped into his local store to buy a length of 2x2 planed timber to finish off a stud wall he was erecting at his Teesside home.

"It didn't really hit me at first", he told us. "I've been buying timber there for years and nothing like this has ever happened. I just picked this bit up off the top of the rack, closed one eye and looked down its length - more out of habit than anything else. When I saw it was straight, I couldn't believe it. I checked it again, then turned to my wife and said "You're not going to believe this, but I think we've got a straight bit"

Mingepiece

George's wife Lillian was so shaken that she almost collapsed and had to sit down on a nearby display of patio chairs. "I was trembling like a leaf", she told reporters later. "You read about people finding straight bits but you never think it's going to happen to you."

Come Bucket

Seconds later George's jackpot joy almost turned to despair when after reaching the checkout he was told the timber didn't have a bar code. The assistant suggested he take it back and get another one. "I was gutted." he said. "But I decided to put my foot down and told them, "No. I'm having this one".

Quim

George and his wife spent the next four and a half hours standing by the till while repeated requests were made over the tannoy for a member of hardware to come to the check out. "By this time the queue was out the shop, across the car park and half way round the local trading estate. But nobody seemed to mind waiting. They all just

Grandad, 72, scoops straight bit of wood

George celebrates with the B&Q store manager

wanted to see my straight bit of wood."

Fadge

Eventually a twelve year old assistant turned up with a stock catalogue and after half an hour located the item in the book. The bar code was then entered into the till manually at the third attempt and George was able to take his wood home.

Fitbin

News of George's good fortune spread quickly and on leaving the store he was mobbed by a crowd of well wishers before being driven away by reporters from a London based tabloid newspaper. Meanwhile in another newspaper a former girlfriend of Mr Clayton has branded him a 'rat', and revealed that handyman George was a flop between the sheets during the couple's stormy two week affair in 1951.

STUDENT GRANT

MONDAY MORNING - FIRST DAY OF TERM. GRANT'S GOT AN 11am LECTURE...

DRONE... DRONE... BLAH... BLAH... DRONE... DRONE...

DRONE... DRONE... BLAH BLAH BLAH DRONE DRONE...

DRONE... DRONE... DRONE... BLAH... BLAH... BLAH BLAH... RHUBARB...

DRI-I-I-NG!

WHACK! WHACK! WHACK! WHACK! WHACKITY-WHACKITY-WHA...

CRASH!

MORNING GWAARNT! HEY! WOOK AT WHAT VEY'RE GIVING AWAY TO THTUDENTTH AT VEH GNAT WETHT BANK VITH TERM!

...ULP...

A FWEE PEETHA VOUCHER... VAWID AT PARTITHIPATING WETHTAUWANTTH BETWEEN THIX AND THIX·FIRTY P/M... EXTHCWUDING WEEKENDTH AND FWIDAYTH. OFFER APPWIETH TO ONE FWEE ONE-INCH FWAT CWUTHT WIV NO TOPPINGTH WHEN YOU BUY EIGHT THIXTHTEEN-INCH DEEP DISTH PEETHATH FOR THE FULL PWITHE.

FREE PIZZA

HMM... ANYWAY, VERE'TH ALTHO A FWEE MIKE FLOWERTH POTTH THEE DEE, THINEMA TICKETTH, POTHTCARDTH, POTHTERTH...

OH- AND VITH THUPERMARKET TWOLLEY AND TWAFFIC CONE.

FACK ME! ALL I GOT FROM MY FACKIN' BANK WAS A SET OF FACKIN' POGS. AND I'D ALREADY GOT SIX OF THEM, ACTUALLY.

RIGHT! I'M OFF TO THE BANK. I'M MOVING MY ACCOUNT TO THE GNAT WEST!

shit.

SHORTLY...

Floyds Bank

FREE POGS FOR STUDENT

HERE- I WANT TO PARLEZ WITH EL MANAGEERO - COMPRENDEREENI? AND I'M TALKIN' ABOUT THE NUMERO UNO HONCHO.

WELL. I'M THE ASSISTANT CLERK WITH RESPONSIBILITY FOR STUDENT BANKING. CAN I BE OF ANY HELP?

NOW LOOK HERE. I'M CLOSING MY ACCOUNT. THEY'RE GIVING AWAY TOP FREEBIES AT THE GNAT WEST.

NOW MR. WANKSHAFT - YOU MUST UNDERSTAND THAT CHANGING YOUR BANK IS NOT A DECISION TO BE TAKEN LIGHTLY.

THERE ARE MANY FACTORS TO BE TAKEN INTO CONSIDERATION.

YOU SHOULD TAKE TIME TO THINK ABOUT FLOYDS BANK'S PREFERENTIAL INTEREST RATE SCHEMES, CASHPOINT AVAILABILITY, 24-HOUR ON-LINE TELEPHONE BANKING, INDEPENDENT FINANCIAL ADVICE, EXTENDED LOAN FACILITIES AND GILT-EDGED ASSET-MANAGEMENT SERVICES.

AND ANYWAY- WE GAVE YOU SOME POGS.

NO. I'M NOT LISTENING TO ANY OF THIS, MR. SQUARE. I'M CLOSING MY ACCOUNT - AND THAT'S AN END TO THE MATTER.

VERY WELL.

I'LL SORT YOU OUT A CLOSING STATEMENT.

RIGHT. THERE'S AN OUTSTANDING BALANCE OF EIGHT-THOUSAND, TWO HUNDRED AND SIX POUNDS EIGHTY-TWO PEE.

YEAH! I'LL SAY IT'S FACKIN' OUTSTANDING. I'LL TAKE IT IN FIFTIES.

NO, MR. WANKSHAFT. YOU DON'T UNDERSTAND. YOU OWE THE BANK OVER EIGHT THOUSAND POUNDS. IT'S CALLED AN OVERDRAFT.

STUDENT BANKING ADVISER

LISTEN, MATEY. YOU MAY THINK YOU'VE WON THIS TIME - BUT YOU HAVEN'T ACTUALLY. YOU'RE DEALING WITH A MEMBER OF THE INTELLECTUAL ELITE. A POLYVERSITY STUDENT. THAT'S RIGHT. I'M IN THE TOP FIFTEEN TO THIRTY-FIVE PERCENT.

AND I'LL TELL YOU SOMETHING ELSE ACTUALLY. I'M NEVER GOING TO JOIN YOUR SAD LITTLE CAPITALIST RAT-RACE IN TWO YEARS' TIME I'LL BE EARNING MORE IN A WEEK THAN YOU'LL SEE IN A FACKING LIFETIME. SO THERE.

ERM... YEAH!

TWO YEARS LATER...

...SO, HERE'S A COPY OF OUR INTRODUCTORY BOOK! - "HEY WOW! - BANKING CAN BE FUN!" OUTLINING ALL OUR SERVICES. HERE'S YOUR POGS...

...AND HERE'S YOUR BALLOON ON A STICK.

WELCOME TO FLOYDS BANK.

Letterbocks

Earthsong? Arsesong more like

❑ **MICHAEL JACKSON prattles on in his latest hit 'Earthsong' about how many animals are being killed on this planet unnecessarily.** Does Mr Jackson have any idea, I wonder, how many laboratory rats, rabbits and hamsters die each year in the interests of cosmetic surgery? I think not. Neither do I, but that's beside the point. In future Mr Jackson should stick to what he knows, and write us a few songs about keeping wild animals as domestic pets, buying off child abuse allegations, fruitcake weddings or being set on fire during TV commercials.

S. Lintel
Canton, Cardiff

Letterbocks,
P.O. Box 1PT,
Newcastle upon
Tyne, NE99 1PT

❑ What is it with posh people that they have to have two second names when everyone else makes do with one? People like Tiggy Legge-Bourke, Lucinda Prior-Palmer and Helen Melons-Windsor. Hats off to Prince Charles for trying to stop this elitist fashion by having no second name at all.

S. Cord
Laira

❑ Why all this song and dance about 'soft drinks' with alcohol in them? What's wrong with kids drinking alcoholic lemonade? The knockers seem to forget that our generation were brought up eating wine gums - available from any sweet shop - and it didn't do us any harm. These po faced spoil sports will want to ban chocolate liqueurs next.

W. Sill
Greensfield, Tyne & Wear

❑ I've been making my own alcoholic lemonade for years. I pour lemonade into a large tumbler, then top it up with half a bottle of gin. Trouble is it tastes too good! By the time my kids get home from school there's never any left.

Mrs J. Irlam
Manchester

Weight a minute...

❑ I don't understand all this fuss about shops having to sell things in metric weights. Kilograms are nearly twice as heavy as pounds, so it looks as if the customer is going to be better off at the end of the day. About time too.

T. Weights
Longsight

❑ I've just seen a film where, after a plane crashed in some mountains, the passengers had to eat each other in order to survive. All well and good, but what do the airlines expect vegetarians like myself to do in similar circumstances? Could scientists clone 'vegetable people', I wonder, a few of whom could travel on every flight to provide a vegetarian alternative to cannibalism in case of disaster.

E. Mullion
Haymarket, Edinburgh

❑ During these recent cold spells we have been plagued with interruptions to our water and electricity supplies. The companies claim that the severe weather took them by surprise. Considering they both sponsor the fucking weather forecasts, perhaps they should go to the trouble of watching one occasionally.

John Tait
Thropton

Turn back the cock

❑ I dread the changing of the clocks each year because it means that for three weeks, until I get used to it, I get my morning stiffy while I'm waiting at the bus stop.

Mark Carnforth
Brighton

Arms race

❑ So, the various Irish paramilitary organisations are still stubbornly refusing to de-commission their weapons. My advise to the British and Irish governments is to suggest 'timing' them, or initiating a 'race' to see who can destroy all their weapons first. This ingenious bluff never fails when my children refuse to do their chores or put their pyjamas on for bed.

Paul Barlow
Wibsey, Bradford

Choca-bollocks

❑ Forest Gumps's mother was talking crap when she said "Life is like a box of chocolates. You never know what you're gonna get". Most chocolates nowadays come with a printed 'menu' telling you exactly what each chocolate contains. "Life is like a bag of Revels" would perhaps have been a more apt expression.

Philip Lowe
Norwich

❑ "And honey I miss you, and I'm being good". Bollocks. Only last week I saw Bobby Goldsboro being sucked off in a car near Leeds bus station by a sour faced old slapper.

Mick McSorley
Beeston, Leeds

Feed the birds vomit and turds

❑ I hear that London restaurants are serving up Trafalgar Square pigeons as top nosh. Why not skip one link in the food chain and simply serve up dog turds and vomit, a typical city pigeon's staple diet.

F. Lance
Glasgow

Happy with my lottery

❑ Who needs a £40 million win on the lottery to find happiness? Up my way £20 will buy seven pints of lager, a kebab and chips and a hand job in the Co-op doorway. I'm a winner every Saturday night.

Bristler Bain
Manchester

❑ Following on from the gentleman who could drink five pints of lager without needing a piss (issue 75). I am a girl, and I can drink ten bottles of Diamond White without throwing up, falling over or starting to cry.

A.L.Nicholson
Wolverhampton

❑ **Is it true that water goes down a plughole in a clockwise spiral North of the Equator, and the opposite way round in the South? If so, why? And what happens if your bath sits directly on the Equator?**

Mr H. Alexander
Pontefrct, West Yorkshire

❑ *Don't ask me Mr Alexander. I'm dead.*

❑ **Why is it that my fingertips wrinkle like prunes if I am in the bath for more than ten minutes?**

Mrs J. Pinder
Oxford

❑ *There's a very simple answer to that Mrs Pinder, but I'm afraid I'm still dead.*

DOCTOR. MY WIFE HAS MISSED HER PERIOD

I'M SURE I SET THE COORDINATES FOR 1872

TOP TIPS

FARTING in bed a problem? Before you hit the sack, try popping a Mint Imperial up your Marmite motorway. That way your guffs will smell good enough to eat.

Sue Denim
London NW1

SAVE a fortune on laundry bills. Give your dirty shirts to Oxfam. They will wash and iron them and you can then buy them back for fifty pence.

J. B. Cartland
Brighton

IGNORE signs in hotel bathrooms telling you to put the shower curtain inside the bath. It takes 28 minutes to get the hooks off.

J. B. Cartland
Brighton

FROZEN drop scones make handy coasters for hot drinks. By the time you finish your drink, the scones should have thawed and will be warm enough to add hot butter and jam.

N. Thorpe
Hockley

WHEN embarking on a new relationship always lend your partner twenty quid. That way, when you inevitably get chucked, at least you get your money back thus cheering up an otherwise miserable day.

A. Rolph
Chelmsford

DON'T waste hundreds of pounds having that tattoo of an ex girlfriend's name removed from your arm by laser surgery. Simply give your new girlfriend £51 and she can have her name changed legally by deed poll to the name on the tattoo.

E.Wolliston
Tottenham

GALAXY 'Minstrels' joined together by a cocktail stick would make a perfect set of dumbbells for a squirrel, if they were a bit bigger. And heavier.

Leigh Loveday
Tamworth

JELLY from pork pies, once warmed up, can be easily spread using a brush and is an economical substitute for varnish on doors, cupboards and skirting boards.

Lee & Dogs
Cleveland

WHEELIE bins left at the gate make ideal shopping trolleys for burglars.

John Tait
Thropton

MAKE motorists sweat for up to ten days. Sit inside a cardboard box on top of a stick at the side of the road and take a flash photo of every car as it goes past.

Alan Currie
Wylam

KEEP your wife on her toes. Nail the housekeeping money to the ceiling.

S. Round
Paignton

CREATE an 'Arctic' scene for your white mice by covering the floor of their cage in talcum powder instead of sawdust, and building a small igloo using sugar cubes.

Dr M. Best
Loughborough

GET your girlfriend to suck a Sterident tablet whilst giving you a blow job. Not only will it give her a dazzling smile, your bell end will come out Bristol fashion.

J. T.
Thropton

NOEL EDMONDS. Rekindle that original element of surprise on your House Party programme by dropping pigs blood instead of coloured foam onto celebrity guests.

Hapag Lloyd
Runcorn

POT HOLERS. Save the emergency services time and money by pot holing in your own bathroom at night. With the lights off, crawl through a bath full of water, under the sink, then get your head stuck in the toilet. Wait till morning for your wife to wake up and 'rescue' you.

J. Moss
Washington

WEATHER men. Save a fortune in meteorological expenses by simply saying that the weather will be the same as it was the day before. More often than not you'll be right.

P. Beading
Thornaby, Cleveland

MUMS. A strip of banana peel tacked to the bottom of children's shoes allows them to be towed effortlessly around supermarkets.

J. Tait
Thropton

TOWNIES. Whenever you see country folk driving into town in their green Range Rovers to go shopping, jump up and down screaming "Get off my land!" Then shoot their dog.

Y. Pages
Cheshire

BURGLARS. Spend half an hour in a hot bath before you do your next 'job'. After a good soak the police will never be able to identify your crinkly fingerprints, or 'dabs'.

Thora Pee
Pontefract

LADIES. Check both your breasts are the same size by making a plaster mould of each. Fill both moulds with water, then pour the contents into two separate measuring jugs. The amounts of water in each will tell you which 'jug' is the bigger.

Mr S. Brown
Peckham

AVOID endless arguments with your wife about leaving the toilet seat down by simply pissing in the sink.

A. Toplight
Neville Hill

DISTURBED American teenagers. Develop a more balanced perspective on life by listening to Ozzie Osborne's 'Suicide Solution' immediately followed by Queen's 'Don't Try Suicide'.

Boogie
Rhonda

A WIRE brush makes an ideal bed of nails for a hamster.

John Tait
Thropton

RAVERS. Pop a wooden spoon in your mouth when dancing. This will eliminate the risk of biting off your tongue in the event of an epileptic fit caused by strobe lighting, and will soon become a fashion item.

W. Brooks
Somerset

WEAR trousers back to front. That way you'll never get the 'little fella' caught in your zip.

G. Adams
Croydon

PROLONG the life of leather underpants by spraying them with 'Scotch Guard' before use.

N. Thorpe
Hockley

I WON A TENNER ON THE LOTTERY AGAIN THIS WEEK.

ITS NOT FAIR. I ALWAYS GET A TICKET BUT I'VE NEVER WON ANYTHING.

YEAH. HOW COME HIS NUMBERS ALWAYS COME UP?

JUST THE LUCK OF THE DRAWER I SUPPOSE.

23

A UNIQUE TRIBUTE TO THE GOLDEN ERA OF THE EIGHTIES

The Murray Mint Gallery, internationally renowned purveyors of nick-nackery present

"GOLD" The Tony Hadley Fabergé Pineapple

The eighties was a decade of affluence and excitement - glamour and glitz - an era of wine bars and sophistication - a decade of decadence lifted aloft by the soldiers of song who marched with the New Romantics. And no braver soldier was there than Tony Hadley out of Spandau Ballet - a bohemian bard whose hits 'Spand' ten immortal years that have now died. But yet they live forever in the form of this beautiful, nice quality pineapple. This heirloom quality ornament by internationally acclaimed fruit jeweller Hercule Poisson-Bleu forms a unique and indestructible' tribute to those times.

"Gold... always believe in your soul"

Externally each faux fruit detail has been hand crafted in solid gold* and bedecked of pearls, perched atop a purest mahogany plinth. It's splendour can only be matched by the quilted silken interior. Open the gold* hinged lid to reveal the stunning golden* figurine of Tony himself, holding his bejewelled microphone aloft. Hand made in breath taking detail, and resplendent in a miniature suit woven of pure platingum, the quality of this piece must be seen to be believed. Subscribe to this exclusive offer immediately and the Tony Hadley 'Gold' Faberge Pineapple could be yours for just £29.95.

ACTUAL SIZE AND APPEARANCE MAY VARY DRASTICALLY FROM ILLUSTRATION.

DETAIL OF TONY HADLEY FIGURINE.

Rosswell Stiles and his INTRIGUING 'X' FILES

MY NAME IS ROSSWELL STILES. AND IN THIS FILING CABINET ARE MY HIGHLY CONFIDENTIAL 'X' FILES

WITHIN THIS VERTICAL SUSPENSION FILING SYSTEM I INTEND TO MAKE A RECORD OF THE UNEXPLAINED. TO OBSERVE THE PARANORMAL. TO REGISTER, IN STRICT ALPHABETICAL ORDER, BIZARRE OCCURENCES AND ALL MANNER OF STRANGE PHENOMENUMS!

AND SO MY SEARCH BEGINS; FOR FALLING FISH, LIGHTS IN THE SKY, CROP CIRCLES, BIG CATS, SPONTANEOUS COMBUSTIONS, BIZARRE DEATHS, ALIEN ABDUCTIONS, ETC. ETC. ETC.

HEAVE! TRUNDLE! TRUNDLE! SQUEAK! SQUEAK! SQUEAK!

SHORTLY... HEY! I CAN'T BELIEVE IT! FISH ARE FALLING FROM THE SKY!

FLOP! FLUMP! FLIP!

A BIZARRE AND QUITE INEXPLICABLE PHENOMENUN...

I'LL RAISE A FILE AND MAKE AN ENTRY UNDER 'F' FOR FALLING FISH!

EXCUSE ME. COULD YOU GET OUT OF THE WAY. I'M TRYING TO FEED THESE SEALS

OH DEAR. LOOKS LIKE I'VE STRAYED INTO THE SEAL ENCLOSURE AT THE LOCAL ZOO!

"HONK!" "HONK!" "HONK!"

PERHAPS I'LL FIND SOME SLIGHTLY MORE MYSTERIOUS INCIDENTS OCCURING IN IN THE PARK

HEAVE! CREAK! RUMBLE! PARK

PHEW! THESE 'X' FILES ARE HEAVIER THAN I'D ANTICIPATED. I THINK I'LL SETTLE DOWN HERE ON THIS BENCH AND WAIT FOR SOMETHING PHENOMINAL TO OCCUR

HUM! HUM!

FUNNY! SNIFF! SNIFF! I CAN SMELL BURNING

YIKES! THAT MAN IS ON FIRE!!

WHOOSH!

BRILLIANT! SPONTANEOUS HUMAN COMBUSTION. HE FRIED TO A CRISP RIGHT BEFORE MY EYES! THIS IS AN PHENOMENA TOTALLY BEYOND SCIENTIFIC EXPLANATION

'FRAID NOT SON!

THERE'S A SIMPLE EXPLANATION. THIS METHS SODDEN TRAMP WAS SATURATED WITH ALCOHOL. EVEN HIS PISS WAS HIGHLY FLAMMABLE. THE BOOZED UP OLD BEGGAR NO DOUBT IGNITED HIMSELF BY CARELESSLY DISCARDING AN OLD FAG END WHICH HE FOUND IN THE GUTTER

SPONTANEOUS HUMAN COMBUSTION INDEED! HO HO HO!

BAH! THERE WAS A PERFECTLY LOGICAL EXPLANATION

LATER... SHHH! I'VE SPOTTED AN 'ABC'- OR ALIEN BIG CAT, WITH MY BINOCULARS!

IT'S OVER BY THAT TREE. PROBABLY STALKING SHEEP

YES, IT'S AN ABC ALRIGHT. A LARGE, WILD FELINE SUCH AS A LEOPARD OR PANTHER, ALIEN TO THE ENVIROMENT IN WHICH IT IS FOUND...

MY GOODNESS, THIS ONE'S HUGE! BIGGER THAN THE BEAST OF BODMIN MOOR! HA! I'D LIKE TO SEE THE SCIENTIFIC WORLD COME UP WITH A RATIONAL EXPLANATION FOR THIS TOTALLY INEXPLICABLE PHENOMENEE

WELL, I'D SAY THAT'S A SMALL KITTEN STANDING NEXT TO A BONSAI TREE, AND YOU'VE GOT YOUR BINOCULARS THE WRONG WAY ROUND

BAH! A SCIENTIST "MEOW!"

FUCKING HELL. THERE'S GOT TO BE SOMETHING AROUND HERE WHICH IS BIZARRE OR PARANORMAL, AND BEYOND THE REALMS OF RATIONAL EXPLANATION

TRUNDLE! RATTLE! CLATTER! CLANK! TO THE COUNTRYSIDE

AHA! THIS COULD BE IT!

CROP CIRCLE TO VIEW £1.00 FARMER

CONTINUED OPPOSITE.

It's a MIRACLE!

Christ appears in pool of vomit

Dinosaur NEWSdesk

JESUS is back. And that's official. For an amazing vision of Christ has appeared in a puddle of sick on the pavement outside a pub in Scarborough.

EXCLUSIVE

The miracle - for that is what it is - occurred last Sunday as unemployed abattoir technician Frank Higgins was enjoying a few quiet lunchtime pints. After drinking eight or nine lagers suddenly his life was changed.

Rough

"I'd had a few the night before and was feeling rough so I ate a couple of pickled eggs and some pork scratchings. Suddenly I got the helicopters so I headed for the door. I only just got outside when I puked up".

Green

It was at that moment the miracle vision occurred. For after gazing at his sick for a few moments, Frank then looked at the wall. Slowly the image of Christ began to appear before his eyes, staring right at him. Frank staggered home to get his camera and managed to take this remarkable picture of the vomit puddle just before the pub landlord swilled it away with a bucket of hot water. And now his incredible photograph is amazing sci-entists and religious lead-ers around the world.

Fairway

"Yes, I can definitely see Jesus", said the Pope after looking at our picture. "Yeah. It's good that. I'd never actually seen him before". The Bishop of Durham was unavailable for comment. "He's not playing with his cock in them toilets anymore. He's just gone away on holiday for Easter", said a spokesman.

Mr Higgins (above) stared in total bewilderment and utter amazedness at the puke shape (right) which formed on the pavement.

Can you see Jesus in the sick?

THIS is how it works. Drink eight or nine pints of lager then go to bed. Wake up in the morning and have a fried break-fast. Then go to the pub and eat two pickled eggs followed by eight or nine more pints of beer. Stare hard at the photograph for at least 30 seconds. Try to con-centrate on the bits of sweetcorn in the middle. Then quickly focus your eyes on a white wall or ceiling. It might take a few seconds, but, incredibly, a vision of Christ will slowly appear and stare straight back at you. Or you'll throw up. One or the other.

Mad dino disease

Dinosaurs may have died out as a result of an early form of 'mad cow disease' according to scientists. There is evidence that some dinosaurs may have gone mad after eating con-taminated offal. Foss-ilised remains of a Brontosaurus dressed as Napoleon were discovered in the Nevada desert in 1994, and DNA tests have shown that a Pleisiosaur unearthed in Africa last year thought it was a teapot.

Dinosaurs wore suits

Dinosaurs may have worn clothes, according to new scientific research. US scientists have discovered fragments of clothing on dinosaur remains in Alaska. Initial reconstruc-tions of the material which had been preserved in mud suggests that the giant reptiles wore baggy suits, not unlike the 'zoot suits' fashionable in America during the thir-ties.

THE ALL-NEW
ADVENTURES OF Billy the Fish

DESPITE BEING BORN HALF-MAN, HALF-FISH, YOUNG BILLY THOMSON HAD MADE THE GOALKEEPER'S JERSEY AT PREMIER LEAGUE LEADERS FULCHESTER UTD. HIS OWN.

FULCHESTER MANAGER TOMMY BROWN HAS BEEN CALLED IN TO SEE CHAIRMAN SIR WINYARD HALL...

YOU WANTED TO SEE ME SIR JOHN. I MEAN SIR WINYARD.

YES TOMMY. IN A SENSE THAT IS CORRECT.

I HAVE A VISION, TOMMY. OF A SPORTING CLUB OF FULCHESTER - TO RIVAL THE GREATEST CLUBS IN EUROPE.

SOUNDS GREAT.

YESTERDAY, I PURCHASED A DOZEN McLAREN F1 SPORTS CARS AND ENTERED THEM IN THE 1996 KENTUCKY FIVE THOUSAND DESTRUCTION DERBY. I HAVE ALSO ASTUTELY SECURED THE SERVICES OF TOP DRIVER ANDREW RIDGELY TO HEAD THE RACING TEAM.

THE RACE IS BEING TELEVISED LIVE - AND IT'S JUST STARTING...

...AND! THEY'RE! OFF!

VROOOM! SCREEEECH! SMASH! BANG!

TINKLE

WELL. IN A SENSE, THAT WAS A MOST SPECTACULAR AND EXPENSIVE TWO MINUTES OF ENTERTAINMENT. BUT IT'S PUT FULCHESTER WELL AND TRULY ON THE INTERNATIONAL SPORTING MAP.

CLICK

IN A VERY REAL SENSE, I HAD MORE MONEY THAN SENSE. BUT IN A SENSE THAT'S NO LONGER THE CASE.

NOW, I HAVE MORE SENSE THAN MONEY. AND IN A VERY REAL SENSE, VERY LITTLE OF EITHER.

...SO MY NEXT GOAL IS TO START BRITAIN'S VERY FIRST CIDER-DRINKING CENTRE OF EXCELLENCE, BRINGING REGENERATION AND PROSPERITY TO THE AREA NEXT TO SOME BINS BENEATH THE RAILWAY ARCHES.

BUT I WON'T STOP THERE. I INTEND TO INCORPORATE AN INTERNATIONAL CLUB OF TROUSER PISSING - AND WITHIN 3 YEARS, A WORLD-RENOWNED CENTRE FOR INCOHERENT SHOUTING.

WELL TOMMY. SIR WINYARD'S MILLIONS HAVE ALL GONE. WE'RE STONY BROKE. WHAT ARE WE GOING TO DO?

WE NEED A NEW BENEFACTOR. SOMEONE PREPARED TO PLOUGH MONEY INTO FULCHESTER UNITED FOOTBALL CLUB.

KNOCK KNOCK!

AH. THAT'LL BE A BENEFACTOR PREPARED TO PLOUGH MILLIONS INTO FULCHESTER UNITED FOOTBALL CLUB.

I'LL GET IT.

GOSH. IT'S PINT-SIZED WANK MAGNATE DIDDY O'SULLIVAN. AND HIS MINDER.

HELLO.

I'M TAKING OVER THIS CLUB - AND I HEREBY APPOINT A GLAMOROUS DOLLY-BIRD TO FLASH HER PINS AND RUN THE BUSINESS.

I'D LIKE YOU TO MEET YOUR NEW BOSS...

OBSCURED ON LEGAL ADVICE

PHWOOAR! I WOULDN'T CLIMB OVER HER TO GET TO YOU SID.

YEAH! I WOULDN'T MIND A BIT OF THAT!

THE NEXT DAY, AT A HASTILY ARRANGED PRESS CONFERENCE...

OBSCURED ON LEGAL ADVICE

MRS. BRADY - WHAT ARE YOUR PLANS FOR FULCHESTER UNITED?

WELL, MY FIRST MOVE WILL BE TO APPOINT A NEW CAPTAIN - TO REPLACE BILLY THE FISH. THE NEW CAPTAIN IS A GENTLEMAN FRIEND OF MINE, WHOM I MET AT A WHIST DRIVE RECENTLY.

OBSCURED ON LEGAL ADVICE

HIS NAME IS MAJOR AMOS LEWERTHWAITE.

ERM... HAVE YOU PLAYED MUCH FOOTBALL BEFORE, MAJOR LEWERTHWAITE?

ERM... TO BE HONEST, I'M MORE OF A CRICKET MAN ACTUALLY...ERM...SWUNG THE WILLOW FOR THE REGIMENT A FEW TIMES IN THE PUNJAB, WHAT.

SURELY - SHE CAN'T DO THAT, TOMMY.

I'M AFRAID SHE JUST HAS, SYD. LEWERTHWAITE IS THE NEW TEAM CAPTAIN AND BILLY THE FISH IS ON THE TRANSFER LIST!!

GULP!

BUT... WE HAVE A CHAMPIONSHIP DECIDER TOMORROW - AGAINST ARCH-RIVALS GRIMTHORPE CITY. IT'S A SIX-POINTER!

YES. AND THIS BLOKE HAS NEVER PLAYED FOOTBALL IN HIS LIFE!

...ERM... MORE OF A POLO MAN MYSELF, WHAT...

...BIT OF CROQUET ON THE LAWN, THAT SORT OF THING...

Probably not to be continued in the next issue

28

SOPHIE STRIPTEASE IS BAD *NUDES* FOR QUEEN!

Sex show just what royal doctors DIDN'T order!

WHAT THE DOCTOR SAW. Surgery temperatures would have been sent soaring as this saucy scene was sawed by Sophie's doctor. This tasteful reconstruction was posed by our models Julie Christie and Michael Winner.

STUNNING Royal-to-be Sophie Rhys-Jones has a disgusting sex secret that she's hiding from her Prince Charming. For innocent Edward is unaware of Sophie's shameful and sordid past.

But now the cat is out of the bag. For today we can exclusively reveal that the raunchy redhead once appeared starkers in a doctors surgery. And saucy Sophie has also featured naked in the changing rooms at her local swimming baths.

Curtains

Rhys-Jones will be red faced when the Royals read about her porny past. For news of her bare exposure could mean curtains for her planned engagement to the Prince. And adoring Edward, who is completely besotted with the former schoolgirl, will find the truth about his Princess-in-waiting hard to stomach.

Croutons

Sophie's steamy closed set session with her GP came to light when old medical records were found by undercover reporters after they had been carelessly discarded in a locked filing cabinet at a doctor's surgery in Cardiff. Described by her doctor as an 'examination', it took place six years ago when Sophie was an unknown 18 year old. Feeling rather poorly she booked an appointment to see her family doctor. In the fifteen minute 'consultation' that followed sexy Sophie obliged the doctor by:

★ **STRIPPING** down to her lacy bra and panties behind a screen.
★**LYING BACK** on a black vinyl couch.
★**BREATHING DEEPLY** as the doctor ran his stethoscope across her naked chest
★**GROANING** as he examined her throat.
★**SIMULATING** a cough.

The sex files also reveal that Sophie answered forthright questions about her health using explicit language. Her doctor then

Prince's pal Sophie bared all!

handed her a prescription which he had written by hand. His hand writing was shaky and barely legible. Afterwards Miss Rhys-Jones casually dressed and then left the building via a front exit.

In the wake of Fergie's notorious indiscretions and Princess Di's self confessed infidelity this latest episode is bound to come as yet another embarrassment to the Palace.

Futons

"Bloody hell. The Queen will shit herself when she hears this. All we need is another bleedin' tart joining the Royal family. Fuck me! As if things aren't bad enough already", said an official Palace spokesman last night.

Is THIS woman fit to be QUEEN?

Is Sophie Rhys-Jones fit to be the Queen of England? That's the question we're asking YOU, the public, in the light of revelations about her taking her clothes off.

With three Royal marriages already up the spout should the Queen allow Edward to marry a woman who is prepared to get her kit off at the drop of a doctor's hat? Do we really want the kind of woman who performs lewd lap dances in front of middle aged men as the future Queen of England? Will she be prepared to reign over us, happy and glorious, like in the words of the Queen's song? Or like them other two, will she simply turn round

and shit on us from a height the minute she gets her foot inside the Palace door?

"The question is virtually irrelevant as there are no conceivable circumstances under which Edward's chosen bride could succeed to the throne", expert Royal watcher Andrew Morton told us yesterday. Bollocks. Don't listen to that ponce. What do YOU think? Ring TODAY and have YOUR say.

Unfortunately we haven't got any of them phone lines so you'll just have to ring each other and discuss it amongst yourselves. But drop us a line and let us know what you decide afterwards.

Stink something Symbol!

THE artist formerly known as Prince is really getting up his record company bosses' noses.
For the star currently being referred to as a symbol is set to change his name again. And this time the pint sized popster - favourite colour purple - is set to be known only as a smell!

Fruitcake

Born Arthur Gerald McNab, it was as Prince that the four foot fruitcake rocketed to stardom in the eighties. Three years ago he changed his name to an anonymous squiggle - a cross between the CND logo and a trumpet. Next the notorious nutter plans to drop that, preferring a pong instead. But record company bosses fear the odour could cause confusion among the record buying public.

Flapjack

"It's difficult to put a smell into alphabetical order", warned Edmundo Capp-

acino, head of Warner Brothers Records. He fears a drop in record sales will inevitably follow any such change. "Fans looking for his records might just think someone's farted. And they won't be able to ask the assistants for help unless they can somehow recreate the smell at the right point during the conversation".

Flip-flop

Prince is known to have considered various smells in his search for a new name, including fish. However close friends say the star has settled on a smell which is a bit like creosote.

Tyrannosaurus pets!

ANIMAL welfare groups have blasted a growing trade in dinosaur eggs in Britain.

Prehistoric reptiles are rapidly becoming the latest in novelty pets with garden centres up and down the country selling almost half a million in the six weeks leading up to Christmas last year. But after hatching as cute lizard like creatures the dinosaurs quickly grow into giant meat eating monsters weighing several tons, yet with brains no bigger than a walnut. Expensive to feed and difficult to control, many owners become bored with their brontosaurus or tire of their T rex. Sadly hundreds are abandoned every year and left to roam the streets, endangering not only their own safety but also that of the general public.

Pets

"Dinosaurs are not domesticated animals. They do not make good pets", warned a spokesman for the RSPCA. "People buy these attractive eggs on a whim. To them they're something of a novelty.

"Dinosaur egg trade is no yolk" say RSPCA

Tragic youngster Paul McLintock pictured weeks before the tragedy

But before they know it the egg has hatched and the soon find themselves with a hundred foot long dinosaur on their hands which eats up to 500 pounds of raw meat - or two whole trees - per day".

Step

Tragic father John McLintock bought his son Paul a triceratops egg to replace a hamster which had died. "It was a lovely little thing at first", he told us. "Paul kept it in his bedroom and fed it crickets. But within a week it was too big for its box, and after a month cracks began to appear in the ceiling below."

On the advice of a consultant structural engineer the triceratops was moved to a ground floor room with a concrete floor. But disaster struck one morning when the animal ate Paul. John had no choice but to have the beast destroyed, an all too familiar scenario to the officers of the RSPCA.

Pest

"On one occasion a man tried to flush a Pleisiosaur

Some dinosaurs yesteryear.

down his toilet. It jammed the sewage pipe and the plumber who was called to unblock the drain lost an arm. These are wild prehistoric animals, not pets. They do not belong in captivity", the spokesman told us.

Tesp

Several garden centres we spoke to denied selling dinosaur eggs. However a spokesman for DIY giants B&Q said that if they did stock them they would probably be under Garden Ornaments.

"If you hang on I'll page someone from Gardening. They might be able to help you", we were told. Two hours later we got fed up with waiting and hung up.

Time bandits net £5000

THIEVES escaped with a haul of £5000 yesterday after a daring raid on a building society in Stockport.

Terrified staff were held at gunpoint by two armed men who demanded cash before making their escape in a time machine They were last seen heading towards Manchester at the time of the industrial revolution. Their vehicle was later found abandoned and burnt out in Runcorn at a primative bronze age settlement during an archeological dig in March 1958. Police believe the gang transferred to a second time machine to make good their escape.

Witnesses describe the men as in their late 20s or early 30s. One was tall, unshaven and

By our Crime and Time correspondents Sapphire and Steel

dressed in 19th Century American clothing. He wore a distinctive wide brimmed hat. The other was of stocky build, Roman in appearance and wore body armour and leather sandals, although the police believe these may have been disguises.

Public

A spokesman for Greater Manchester C.I.D. today appealed for members of the public from all periods in time - past, present and future - to come for-

wards - or backwards - if they have any information about the crime. "Someone, somewhere knows - or knew - who these men are. Or were. Or indeed will be. I appeal to them to get in touch. Any information will be treated in the strictest confidence".

Anaesthetic

However he issued a warning to any members of the public who come into contact with the men. "These men are armed and extremely dangerous. I have no doubt that they would use violence if confronted. If you see them you should act quickly and wrestle them to the ground before they get a chance to shoot or stab you."

RIGHT. THAT'S ME SPUDS PEELED. I'LL JUST NIP OUT AND GET SOME CAT FOOD FOR TIDDLES BEFORE I PUT THEM ON THE BOIL.

EEH, LOOK. A NEW SUPERMARKET. THEY'VE PUT THAT UP QUICK. THIS WAS ALL TREES IN MY DAY.

EEH. ITS BLOODY RIDICULOUS THE WAY THEY KEEP MOVING THINGS AROUND. I CAN'T FIND THE CAT FOOD. WELL - THEY CAN BLOODY TICKLE. I'LL GET THE BUS TO KWIKSAVE.

TUPPENNY ONE TO KWIKSAVE. ME PASS IS AT THE BOTTOM OF ME BAG.

THEY NEVER HAD THESE BUSES WHEN I WAS A GIRL. IT WAS ALL TRAMS IN THEM DAYS. THERE WAS ALWAYS ONE WHEN YOU WANTED ONE AND YOU COULD GO RIGHT THE WAY TO THE TERMINUS AND BACK FOR A FARTHING.

MIND YOU THERE WAS NO BANANAS... BUT THAT WAS THE KAISER'S FAULT.

THEY SAID IT WOULD ALL BE OVER BY CHRISTMAS. CHRISTMAS WAS BETTER IN THE OLD DAYS.

WE HAD A WHIP AND TOP AND A DOLL MADE OUT OF COAL. 12 OF US IN A BED, PACKED IN LIKE SARDINES WE WAS.

HAVE YOU SEEN THE PRICE OF SARDINES AT SAINSBURYS - FOURTEEN PEE THATS NEARLY THREE SHILLING. WHEN I STARTED IN SERVICE I DIDN'T GET THREE SHILLING AND THAT WAS A LOT OF MONEY IN THEM DAYS. AND I HAD TO WORK FOR IT.

NOT LIKE TODAY.

...I HAD TO GET UP AT SIX IN THE MORNING AND WALK THREE MILES TO THE TRAM. IT WAS ALL TRAMS IN THEM DAYS. THERE WAS ALWAYS ONE WHEN YOU WANTED ONE AND YOU COULD GO RIGHT THE WAY TO THE TERMINUS AND BACK FOR A FARTHING.

...MIND YOU - THERE WAS NO BANANAS...

NINE HOURS LATER...

...AND I HAD TO WORK FOR IT. NOT LIKE TODAY. I HAD TO GET UP AT THREE IN THE MORNING - NO BREAKFAST MIND - WALK TEN MILES TO THE TRAM...

NEW YORK AIRPORT

RIGHT. NOW WHERE'S KWIKSAVE?

EEH. IT'S CHANGED ROUND 'ERE.

OOH LOOK. THIS WAS ME GRANDAD'S OLD SHOP. SOLD TEA HE DID. LOOSE IN WAX CONES. TUPPENCE FARTHING AND IT WAS BETTER THAN THESE BAGS YOU GET NOWADAYS. Y'CAN TASTE THE PAPER. AND BROKEN BISCUITS.

EMPIRE STATE BUILDING.

HEY LADY. HAND OVER THE FUCKIN' BREAD YOU FUCKIN' MOTHERFUCKER OR I'LL BLOW YO' GODDAMM MOTHERFUCKIN' HEAD OFF.

HAVE THEY STILL GOT MR. CAT ON SPECIAL OFFER AT KWIKSAVE?

SAY WHAT ASSWIPE MOTHERFUCKER?

ONLY HE WON'T HAVE WHISKAS OR CHOOSY.

DON'T YOU FUCKIN' FUCK WITH MY FACE YOU MOTHERFUCKER. JUS' FUCKIN' HAND OVER THE GODDAMM DOUGH, Y'FUCKIN' FUCK.

EEH. THE LANGUAGE.

I COULD VOMIT.

OKAY WISEGUY - SCOOT - OR I'LL RUN YOUR BUTT IN DOWNTOWN TO THE BIG HOUSE!

YEAH?

YEAH.

WELL FUCK YOU!

EEH. THANK GOODNESS - ITS A BOBBY. NOW - WHERE'S KWIKSAVE? YOU SEE I NEED MR. CAT. MY TIDDLES WON'T LOOK AT WHISKAS OR CHOOSY.

GO FUCK YOURSELF LADY. BUY A GODDAMM STREET-MAP. I AIN'T NO GODDAMM PUBLIC INFORMATION SOYVICE.

HOURS LATER...

BERG'S 24 HOUR DRUGS, GUNS, PRETZELS, BAGELS, SASPERILLY, SODYPOP, ORTHODONTABILIA & CAT FOOD.

EEH THERE'S ME BUS. THE NUMBER SIX.

DROP ME OFF RIGHT OUTSIDE ME FRONT DOOR THAT WILL.

...AND THERE WAS ALWAYS ONE WHEN YOU WANTED ONE. AND YOU COULD GO RIGHT THE WAY TO THE TERMINUS AND BACK FOR A TENTH OF AN OLD PENNY...

...MIND YOU, THERE WAS NO EGGS, ALL THE SOLDIERS HAD THEM IN THE TRENCHES AT WIPERS...

NINE HOURS LATER...

EEH. I'LL BE GLAD TO GET INSIDE AND PUT ME FEET UP.

EH? OH DEAR. HE'S GIVE ME THE WRONG FLAVOUR. MY TIDDLES WILL TURN HIS NOSE UP AT THIS.

I'LL HAVE TO TAKE 'EM BACK.

LATER...

...YOU'VE GIVE ME TUNA YOU ARAB. MY TIDDLES ONLY EATS DUCK AND HEART...

WORLD O' TATTOOS

RED SQUARE

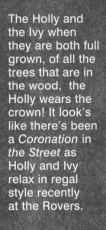

The Holly and the Ivy when they are both full grown, of all the trees that are in the wood, the Holly wears the crown! It look's like there's been a *Coronation* in *the Street* as Holly and Ivy relax in regal style recently at the Rovers.

Thighs to see you, to see you *thighs!* There's no sign of a generation gap between TV's Bruce Forsyth and daughter Danielle on a recent night out, despite the 73 year age difference.

Do ya think I'm specksy?

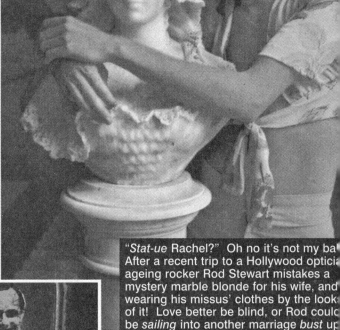

"*Stat-ue* Rachel?" Oh no it's not my ba After a recent trip to a Hollywood optici ageing rocker Rod Stewart mistakes a mystery marble blonde for his wife, and wearing his missus' clothes by the look of it! Love better be blind, or Rod coul be *sailing* into another marriage *bust* up

Donald where's ya troosers? Karaoke kid the late Donald Campbell sings like a Bluebird at a recent bash to celebrate the 25th anniversary of his being '*kilt*' in an ill fated world speed record attempt on Coniston Water.

Whale meat again? Dame Vera Lynn asks Bjork to recommend a dish during a recent visit to an Eskimo restaurant in Soho.

U2 can have a body like mine! There's more to Bono than just skin and bono, as he proved at a recent celebrity weight lifting com petition. The strain was beginning to show but Bono bravely carried on. "Don't stop me cos I'm close to The Edge" he told the judges.

special? Dolph

O-no, does Yoko know you're out? Ex-Beatle John Lennon makes a comeback on the New York party scene with a mystery blonde by his side. *Imagine* he'll be wanting a *stiff* drink after being dead for 16 years.

Where did you get that fat? Evans above! Looks like outsize TFI *Fry-up* star Chris Evans has had too many *Big Breakfasts!* But that hasn't put off one mystery blonde admirer.

Some like it hot! Hollywood veteran Tony Curtis and stunning author Dame Barbara Cartland step out for a curry in Bradford recently. How did Tony *persuade 'er* to do that? At 140 he's old enough to be her Grandad. Oops! Looks like he's pissed his trousers.

"And when the prostitute took my cock in her mouth it was *THIS* big" quips poncey actor Hugh Grant.

Hanks for the mammaries! Super-model Claudia *pops out* - quite literally - with boyfriend Hank Marvin. A *Marvin-ous* sight without a *Shadow* of a doubt!

CELEBRITY NOSE PICS!

"Can I do that for you Your Majesty?" Jeffrey Archer is green nosing with the Royals. Perhaps Di could have picked at a more appropriate moment.

Golfer Jack Nicklaus looks on as his wife Mary aims for the second green. Daughter Danielle has already scored one bogie for par!

America's former First Lady Nancy Regan (above) has picked something special to wear. Hope she's *snot* shaking too many hands today. And Jarvis Cocker's doing it, doing it, doing it. Picking his nose and chewing it, all day long.

34

the SAD SEXIST

IN THE PUB...
RUBBISH!
NAH SID, IT'S TRUE MAN, THE BEST PLACE TU PICK UP BORDS NOWADAYS IS IN THE FUCKIN' SUPERMARKET!

WHAT? SO I JUST GAN TO NETTO?
NOT FUCKIN' NETTO MAN!
WHY, ALDI'S IN GATESHEED, BUT,
YE DIWEN'T FUCKIN' GERRIT MAN SID,... CLASS MAN, ...CLASS... KWIK SAVE.

AYE. YER BEST BET FER TOP MOTT IS AT THE DELICANTESSUN COONTA. YE GAN ROOND AN' FILL UP YA TROLLEY WI' AALL POSH STUFF, FRUIT, VEGTABLES, PASTA... STUFF LIKE THAT PESTURR SAUCE... CHICKEN-THE-NEET AN' THAT.

WATCH YA FUCKIN' MOOTH I'M NAE VORGIN!
AYE. EXTRA VORGIN OLIVE OIL.

THEN Y'HANG AROOND THE DELI COONTA LOOKIN' AT AALL THE BIT KEESH AN' SCOTCH EGGS.
AYE. THEN THE CLASS FANNY'LL BITE!

SO...
DELICATESSE

EXCUSE ME. ARE YOU IN THE QUEUE FOR THE DELICATESSEN?
AYE. D'YU WANNA GAN OOT WI' US?
WELL, I DO KNOW A CHARMING LITTLE EATERY A DEAR FRIEND HAS, CHEZ PIERE. HAVE YOU HEARD OF IT?
ERM...NAH. FUNNY NAME FOR A PUB. HAVE THE' GOT THE BIG SCREEN FOR THE SKY MATCHES?

SO...
EEEH. I COULD EAT A SCABBY MONKEY FRIED IN CLARTS.

I'M SORRY SIR, BUT YOU CANNOT ENTER THE DINING AREA WITHOUT A JACKET.
WHY LIKE? IS YER FUCKIN' HEATIN' BUST?

NO SIR. BUT WE HAVE A STRICT DRESS CODE. WE CAN LEND YOU A DINNER JACKET.
ERM..., AYE, SOONDS CANNY.

SO... HOW! PUT THAT BACK! I WUZ JUST GANNA FUCKIN' SIT ON THAT!

HOW, MATE! YU'V GIVE US TOO MANY KNIVES AN' FORKS... THEZ ONLY TWO O' WU!

YOUR NAPKIN SIR.
HOW! WHAT'S FUCKIN' GANNIN' ON HERE? ARE YE FUCKIN' TRYIN' TU FEEL ME NUTS?!

HOW, MATE! I THINK THE WAITER'S ON THE OTHER FUCKIN' BUS!... ... TRIED TU SKWEEZE ME PODS.

IF SIR AND MADAM WOULD LIKE TO ORDER DRINKS I CAN PARTICULARLY RECOMMEND THE CHATEAUX PAP DE PUTAIN.
ERM... CANNY. AS LANG AS IT'S NOT WAARM WE'LL HAVE A PINT AN' A HALF O' THAT. HOY SOME LIME IN THE BORD'S. AYE. AN' KEEP YER EYES OFF 'ER TITS AN' AALL.

HE'S LOOKIN' AT ME BORD'S TITS NOO!

I CAN RECOMMEND THE FISH MOST HIGHLY.
ERM. AYE, HE'S GIVE US THE WRANG FUCKIN' MENU HERE, THIS 'UNS AALL IN FOREIGN.

LATER... ...AYE, THEN THE VICAR SEZ TU THE DWAARF, "NAH! IT WUZ THE CUCUMBER THAT HAD THE TEETH MARKS IN IT!" ...HAH! HAH! D'YU GERRIT?
AHEM! YOUR FOOD SIR AND MADAM.

EH?

LATER... WELL, WE'LL NOT BE GANNIN' BACK THERE, WILL WU, PET? FAWATY-EIGHT POOND FOR A BAIRN'S PORTION O' FISH WI' NAE CHIPS! AN' THE' DIDN'T EVEN BRING ANY DADDIES' TILL I HAD THAT WAITER AGAINST THE WAALL...FAWATY-EIGHT POOND!... JEESUS!

HOW MUCH DID YE PAY FOR YOURS?

SIDNEY. I'D LIKE TO SAY THAT THIS HAS BEEN ONE OF THE MOST MORTIFYING EXPERIENCES OF MY LIFE. I HAVE NEVER FELT SO DEMEANED OR DEREGATED. I ABHOR AND REVILE YOU. YOU ARE THE MOST ODIOUS PIECE OF DETRITUS THAT IT HAS EVER BEEN MY LAMENTABLE MISCHANCE TO MEET. THE WHOLE EVENING HAS BEEN A CONSUMATE DEBARCLE FROM THE MOMENT WE MET.

EEH WELL, I'M GLAD Y'LIKED IT. SO, WHAT'S ME CHANCE OF A QUICK KNEE-TREMBLER IN THEM BUSHES, PET?

FIN.

GILBERT RATCHET

I LOVE WATCHING CROWN GREEN BOWLING! IT'S THE MOST BRILLIANT SPORT IN THE WORLD

COME ON, THE FAT BLOKE IN THE JUMPER!

COR! IT'D BE A REAL THRILL TO WATCH A **LIVE** BOWLING MATCH

CROWN GREEN BOWLS
TODAY: ADMISSION £1.50

BUT I'VE SPENT ALL MY POCKET MONEY ON POGS

BOO HOO SNIFF

WHAT'S AILING YOU, MISS?

I'M SUPPOSED TO BE TRAINING TO BE A SUPERMODEL

BUT I DAREN'T STICK MY FINGERS DOWN MY THROAT IN CASE THE REGURGITATED GASTRIC JUICES DISSOLVE MY NAIL VARNISH

NEVER FEAR! I'LL SOON RIG YOU UP A SIMPLE BUT EFFECTIVE VOMITING AID

NICE WORK, GILBERT. THIS DEVICE OUGHT TO HELP BRING UP MY ENTIRE STOMACH LINING

PLEASE ACCEPT THIS FIFTY PENCE

HELLO MR STURMEY-ARCHER. YOU LOOK PERTURBED

INDEED I AM, GILBERT...

IN ABOUT 16 HOURS TIME THE LIVELY AND LIGHT-HEARTED TV SHOW 'BUSHELL ON THE BOX' IS DUE ON, FEATURING THE POPULAR LOVEABLE MEDIA PERSONALITY GARRY BUSHELL

I'M TRYING TO DRINK MYSELF UNCONSCIOUS BEFORE THE PROGRAMME STARTS — BUT I'M AFRAID THIS WHISKEY WON'T BE STRONG ENOUGH

IF IT'S OBLIVION YOU'RE AFTER, YOU NEED A DRINK WITH A LITTLE MORE BITE

A COUPLE OF GALLONS OF 4-STAR SYPHONED OUT OF THIS PETROL TANK SHOULD ENSURE THAT YOU MISS THE ENTIRE PROGRAMME

THANKS GILBERT. THIS OUGHT TO SEE ME SAFELY OUT FOR THE COUNT BY THE TIME THAT SHIT-WITTED BIGOTED SHIFTY-EYED CUNT STARTS TWATTING AROUND ON HIS SOFA TRYING DESPERATELY TO BE LADDISH AND OCCASIONALLY PRETENDING TO BE OUTRAGED ABOUT SOMETHING OR OTHER IN AN EMBARRASSINGLY UNCONVINCING WAY

HERE'S 50p

SUPERB! I'VE EARNED A QUID ALREADY

I JUST NEED ANOTHER 50p AND I'LL BE ABLE TO SEE THE CROWN GREEN BOWLS

OOH DEAR. I'VE BEEN STOOD HERE FOR **NINETY SIX** HOURS FEEDING THE DUCKS

BREAD

NOW I'VE GOT REPETITIVE STRAIN INJURY AND AM UNABLE TO THROW ANY MORE BREAD

USING A SIMPLE SEE-SAW MECHANISM, WE CAN FEED ALL YOUR BREAD TO THE DUCKS IN ONE FELL SWOOP

BREAD

BREAD

HEY-HUP!

SPLASH!

YOU BLITHERING OAF! BY SPLASHING ALL THE WATER OUT OF THE POND, YOU HAVE EXPOSED THE CANNISTER OF TOXIC NUCLEAR WASTE WHICH I CAREFULLY DUMPED THIS MORNING

COMEDY PARKIE

TOXIC WASTE

WE CAN'T LEAVE IT THERE HIGH AND DRY. YOU'LL JUST HAVE TO FIND SOMEWHERE ELSE TO DISPOSE OF IT

EXCUSE ME YOUNG MAN. I'M **BAXTER BASICS** YOUR LOCAL M.P., AND I'LL GIVE YOU FIFTY PENCE FOR THAT BARREL OF TOXIC WASTE

TOXIC WASTE

IT'S JUST WHAT I NEED FOR MY PHOTO-OPPORTUNITY WITH THE NATIONAL PRESS THIS AFTERNOON

IT IS QUITE CLEAR TO ME THAT TOXIC WASTE IS PERFECTLY SAFE. MY OWN FAMILY EATS TOXIC WASTE AND I HAVE NO WORRY ABOUT THAT. AS YOU CAN SEE, MY 4-YEAR OLD DAUGHTER SIMPLY WOLFS IT DOWN.

GLUG GLUG GLUG GLUG

TOXIC WASTE

TOXIC WASTE IS AS BRITISH AS YORKSHIRE PUDDING, AND THERE IS NO EVIDENCE THAT IT IS IN ANY WAY HARMFUL

WHOOPEE! NOW I'VE EARNED ENOUGH FOR THE CROWN GREEN BOWLS

WAY IN

CROWN GREEN BOWLS
TICKETS £1.50

AND NOW FOR THE PUNCHLINE, EH READERS?

RIGHT. ERM. THIS PUNCHLINE DOESN'T MAKE MUCH SENSE, BUT ANYWAY... I HEREBY **CROWN** YOU WITH THIS **GREEN BOWL** OF FRUIT!

OH NO! IT'S **THAT** SORT OF "CROWN GREEN BOWLS"

GREEN
GREEN
1st PRIZE
2nd PRIZE

OR SOMETHING

FUCKING HELL

READER'S VOICE

ROGER HAS BEEN CALLED IN AT THE LAST MINUTE TO PRESENT 'TOPGEAR' AFTER REGULAR HOST JEREMY CLARKSON FAILED TO TURN UP FOR WORK...

NOW REMEMBER ROGER, THIS PIECE TO CAMERA SHOULD BE DONE IN A 'LADDISH' STYLE... RACEY AND NEAR THE KNUCKLE

THINK HOW JEREMY CLARKSON WOULD DO IT... YOU KNOW, HE'S A BIT OUTSPOKEN... HE SAILS CLOSE TO THE WIND... A TOUCH ON THE SEXIST SIDE. POLITICALLY INCORRECT

I DON'T KNOW ABOUT THIS, TOM... IT'S NOT ME AT ALL. I KNOW I'M AN ACTOR, BUT... I'M NOT COMFORTABLE WITH IT

IT'S, ERM... FIVE GRAND FOR THE ONE HALF HOUR SHOW, ROGER

OKAY, EVERYBODY, 3...2...1... AND **ACTION**!

TODAY, MY DREAM HAS COME TRUE... I'VE BEEN INVITED TO TEST DRIVE THE FERRARI TESTOSTEROSSA

UNDER THE BONNET, THERE'S THE HORSE POWER OF 800 ITALIAN STALLIONS, CHOMPING AT THE BIT, READY FOR TAKE OFF, AND FROM NAUGHT TO SIXTY IN 1·7 SECONDS. IT'S FASTER OFF THE BLOCKS THAN CONCORD

LOOK AT IT. A TON OF THROBBING RED STEEL. PURE TROUSER BURSTING POWER

AND WHAT A SHAPE. IT'S GOT MORE CURVES THAN A PLAYBOY CENTREFOLD

...YOU KNOW... IF THIS CAR WAS A BIRD... I'D FUCK ITS ARSE OFF...

...AND COME ALL OVER ITS TITS

FUCK IT! I THINK I **WILL**! COME HERE, YOU HORNY ITALIAN **BITCH**!

CUT!!

YEAH! URGH! URGH! URGH! YEAH! THAT'S IT!

ROGER!

JESUS CHRIST, ROGER! CALM DOWN WILL YOU!

ERM... THAT WAS GOOD ROGER, BUT I THINK YOU WENT A LITTLE **TOO** FAR

WHAT? TOO **SEXY**? I COULD LOSE THE REFERENCE TO PLAYBOY IF YOU LIKE

ACTUALLY, I THINK IT MIGHT BE BEST IF WE STICK TO THE TECHNICAL DETAILS... LOOK AT THE VARIOUS FEATURES

ANYTHING YOU SAY TOM

SO... BOOT! TAKE ONE. **ACTION**!

WELL, YOU DON'T EXPECT TO FIT A SOFA IN THE BACK OF A THOROUGHBRED SPORTS CAR...

...BUT EVEN SO, BY ANY STANDARDS, THE LUGGAGE SPACE IS DISSAPPOINTINGLY SMALL

...I MEAN... FOR **FUCK'S SAKE** WHO ARE THEY TRYING TO KID?

YOU COULD GET MORE SUITCASES IN MOTHER THERESA'S FANNY THAN IN THERE

CUT!

WHAT'S WRONG, TOM? WAS THERE A HAIR IN THE GATE?

NO. LOOK, LET'S GO STRAIGHT ONTO THE TEST DRIVE, ROGER

TEST DRIVE?

WHAT... YOU MEAN ON THE ROAD?

YEAH! DRIVE THROUGH A COUPLE OF NICE PICTURESQUE VILLAGES, OVERTAKE THE CAMERA CAR...

ERM...

...SPIN THE WHEELS ON SOME GRAVEL, GO ROUND A CORNER, THAT SORT OF THING... DUB SOME MUSIC ON AFTER

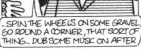

BIT OF A PROBLEM THERE, TOM. YOU SEE... I'VE LOST MY LICENCE AGAIN

WHAT?

YEH. DEATH BY RECKLESS DRIVING...

...HIT A BUS QUEUE. CAME OUT OF FUCKIN' NOWHERE... THIER FAULT ENTIRELY

NOT TO WORRY, TOM. I GET IT BACK IN 2002. WE CAN FILM IT THEN AND CUT IT IN LATER

NO, ROGER. THIS IS BROADCAST ON FRIDAY. 2002 IS FIVE YEARS AWAY

IS IT? **FUCK**! HOW AM I GOING TO GET TO THE PUB?

SUDDENLY...

SORRY I'M LATE. I'VE JUST BEEN WRITING MY COLUMN FOR EVERY PAPER IN THE COUNTRY

AH! PHEW! MR. CLARKSON. I'M **SO** GLAD YOU'RE HERE!

RIGHT! FIRST, CAN WE DO A LITTLE INTRODUCTORY PIECE TO CAMERA? WE'RE ALL SET UP OVER HERE

NO PROBLEM

SO... TAKE 2... **ACTION**!

WHAT'S YOUR **DREAM** CAR?

E-TYPE JAG? PORCHE 911? AUSTIN MARTIN DB7?

MINE IS THE FERRARI TESTOSEROSSA... THIS IS ONE HERE...

...AND THESE...

ARE THE **KEYS**!

BUT I'M NOT GOING TO DRIVE THIS BEAUTY...

...I'M GOING TO **FUCK** IT...

UP THE ARSE!

YEAH! TAKE THAT, YOU SEXY BITCH. IT'S **HARD** URGH! OOH! YOU **LOVE** IT, DON'T YOU. URGH! URGH!

OOH, YEAH!

MARVELOUS, ISN'T HE?!

YES. HE'S SUCH A LAD

I LOVE HIS HUMOUROUS COLUMNS. THEY'RE SO OUTSPOKENLY OPINIONATED

JOHNNY FARTPANTS

LUMBER-LAUGHS A-PLENTY WITH YOUR FLATULENCE FUNNIES FAVOURITE

PHRUTT!

OH DEAR!

OUR SHINY BUGLE HAS BEEN STOLEN BY A MAGPIE. NOW I CAN'T PLAY REVEILLE.

DON'T WORRY AKELA, I'LL BRING THE TROOP TO ORDER BY BLOWING A FARTFARE OUT MY ARSE.

SUPER!

DA-DA-DIDDLE-DEE!
DA-DA-DIDDLE-DEE!
DA-DA-DIDDLE-DEE!
DA-DAAAAH-DOH!
DA-DA-DIDDLE-DEE!
DA-DA-DIDDLE-DEE!
DA-DA-DIDLE-DEE!
DA-DAAAAH!

WELL DONE JOHNNY! AN EXCELLENT RUMPET VOLUNTARY, YOU'VE CALLED THE PACK TO ORDER...

... AND EARNED YOUR RECTAL CONTROL BADGE TO BOOT!
COR! THANKS!

RIGHT BOYS, THE GANGSHOW IS TOMORROW NIGHT, AND LORD BADEN-POWELL IS ATTENDING AS OUR GUEST OF HONOUR.
COR!
WOW!

SO I WANT YOU ALL TO PRACTICE YOUR ACTS. ALL THE PROPS YOU WILL NEED IS BACKSTAGE.

I'M GOING TO DEMONSTRATE HOW TO START A FIRE BY RUBBING TWO STICKS TOGETHER.
PROPS

GREAT IDEA! I THINK I'LL DO SOME CONJURING TRICKS!
AND I'M GOING TO DO SOME TYING OF NOVELTY KNOTS TO MUSIC.

WHAT ARE YOU GOING TO DO JOHNNY?
YEAH? WHAT'S THAT THEN?
WELL, I INTEND TO TAKE BADEN-POWELL BACK TO AFRICA ON A SAFARTI OF SOUND.
I'LL SHOW YOU.

AHEM! DAWN BREAKS OVER THE SERENGHETT! AND THE FIRST TO WAKE IS A FLANGE OF BABOONS, WHO WHOOP EXCITEDLY AT SOME BANANAS UP A TREE.

WHOOP!
WHOOP!
WHOOP!

MEANWHILE AT THE WATERHOLE, A CHORUS OF BULLFROGS SERENADE THE SHIMMERING SUN.
BLOIK!
BLOIK!
BLOIK!

AND FINALLY, WE SURPRISE A ROGUE BULL-ELEPHANT IN THE BUSH, WHO RAISES HIS TUSKS IN ALARM AND BELLOWS AT THE TOP OF HIS VOICE.

GNNNNN!
LOOK EVERYONE! THEY'RE STARTING TO SPARK!

BOOM!

WELL JOHNNY, LOOK AT THE DAMAGE YOU'VE CAUSED, I'LL HAVE TO PHONE LORD BADEN-POWELL AND TELL HIM THAT THE CONCERT IS CANCELLED.
DON'T WORRY AKELA.

WE'VE GOT THESE OUT-OF-DATE, PART-THAWED CATERING PACKS OF BERNARD MATTHEWS TURKEY DRUMMERS...
... AND THAT MEANS WE'VE GOT A SHOW!
Bernard Matthews TURKEY DRUMMERS

WE'RE RIDING ALONG ON THE CREST OF A FART, AND THE METHANE STINGS OUR EYES, OUR NOSES HAVE PEGS ON, THAT FART IT HAD LEGS ON, LOOK OUT YOU PASSERS-BY...
... HIS RING IT IS STINGING, BUT WHILE HE FARTS WE'LL KEEP SINGING...
MUNCH! CHOMP!
... WE'RE RIDING ALONG ON THE CREST OF A FART, AND IT SMELLS OF EGGS!!

You know that Mr. *Squeaky Clean*, Richard Branson? Guess how he made his money? I'll tell ya. Abortions. Yeah, *doing abortions!* Seen 'im on the telly I did. He didn't 'ave a beard, but it was definitely 'im. Doing abortions he was, on girls. That's where the name come from, Virgin. Straight up.

I'll tell you whose got mad cow disease. Harry Enfield. Poor bloke. *Mad as a hatter he is.* Locked himself in his house a year ago, hasn't been out since. Never see him on the telly any more, do ya? That's why. They reckon everyone'll 'ave it in 5 years.

It's no wonder women get pissed so easy. It's cos their *organs* are so small. I read it in a book. Our organs are *seven times* bigger than theirs. They can't absorb as much alcohol you see. Smaller organs.

You know Rod Stewart's had his whole face lifted, don't ya? *All of it.* They've stretched it so far, right, he has to *shave* behind his ears. No, *honest* - it's true that. You look at him next time he's on the box. Stubble behind 'is ears. You should ask Joanna Lumley, eh? *Wink wink!* She'd know.

If you sleep with your head next to your fuse box you get CANCER. Smokin's actually *good* for you. That's what they reckon. It's electricity that causes cancer. Pylons an' that. Mate of mine's wife cooked her tits sittin' next to a microwave. Bloody lethal those things.

'Ere! Daley Thompson, right, won the Olympics? He's met *aliens* from another planet. Yeah! Mate of mine's friend's a reporter. He told him, *strictly off the record.* Straight from the 'orses mouth. He even speaks their language. Knows all their *terminology* an' that. Course, he's keepin' it a secret. Doesn't want everyone to *panic*, y'see.

Did you know that your ears are the only bit of you that never stop growing? Even when you're old. That's why old blokes always have *huge* big ears. It's true that. You think about it.

Ever been to a sperm bank? No? I'll tell you what. *You wanna try it mate!* Mind, there's no wanking. Nah, nah, nah. It's all *clinical*, y'see. The nurse, right, she knows exactly what to do. She just sticks her finger up your arse, and gives the old walnut a poke. *Bang!* Off you go. *Instant* it is. Take's less than a second.

Spectres spooked by Big 'C' scare

GHOSTS were turning white with fear last night after new evidence emerged suggesting a possible link between walking through walls and cancer.

Doctors fear that wall cavity insulation - the expanding foam substance used to insulate walls - could be hazardous when walked through. And that's bad news for phantoms at haunted houses all over Britain, many of whom could already have been exposed to serious risk.

Popular

In recent years wall cavity insulation has become an increasingly popular form of home improvement. Householders keen to shave a few pennies off their fuel bills pay extortionate amounts for a foam solution to be pumped into the hollow cavity within the external walls of their property. This then expands and hardens to form a heat retaining membrane within the wall. They hope.

Prefect

But researchers now believe there is strong evidence linking an increasing number of ghost cancers with the use of the foam. Statistics show that in the last twenty years cases of ghost cancer have almost trebled, with an estimated 2,000 ghosts dying each year from cancer related illness.

Head boy

Silus Hodgson was murdered by highwaymen in a field in 1730. His ghost haunted the spot where he died for over 200 years until a house was built on it in 1937. He then began haunting the house. All was well until 1982 when a new owner had the walls insulated. Twelve years later Mr Hodgson's ghost was looking at its stomach, which is see through, when it noticed a lump. Shortly afterwards doctors diagnosed an inoperable stomach tumour and Mr Hodgson's ghost was given only six months to live. Less than five months later it was dead again.

Mr Hodgson's ghost's ghost outside the house he had haunted.

Now haunting the spot where his ghost died, Mr Hodgson's ghost's ghost believes the people who manufacture and install the foam should be held responsible. "There is a clear case of negligence to be answered. No cautionary measures were taken - no warnings were put on the walls - and as a result my life and the lives of numerous other ghosts have been cut short", it told us.

We rang a solicitor who advertises free initial consultations in the local newspaper but his knowledge of the law as it applied to ghosts was flimsy to say the least. We then rang Mr Gill, a builder who did some work at our office five years ago, but he told us he didn't believe in ghosts. And he doesn't do wall cavity insulation either.

Real-life Royal photo-romance in...
DIANA: PRINCESS OF HEARTS

Her true story by Andrew Motherwell   Photography by Lord Snowman

Congratulations Lady Spencer. It's a Princess.

Wonderful. We'll call her Di. Lady Di.

Althorp Estate, a prestigious development of luxury 3 and 4 bedroom executive detached houses set in the Norfolk countryside. Home to the Spencer family; father Earl and his wife Lady who, on July 1st 1961, were celebrating a new addition to the family.

The Spencer's were well off, and as a child Di wanted for nothing.

Look, one has got you a Crown Jewels rattle

Gar gar! goo goo!

Already she was showing signs of being a Princess of Hearts, and the young Diana spent much of her time in the kitchen making some tarts.

One day ay shell be the Queen. The Queen of Hearts!

But, at the tender age of four, Diana's heart was broken when her mother ran off with a wallpaper salesman.

Please don't go, mommy. Don't go away and leave us.

Ay em sorry children, but ay em in love with Mr Shand, the wallpaper salesman. We must be orf now. Goodbye.

Earl re-married, but Diana hated her wicked stepmother, the millionaire centenarian pulp romantic novelist Dame Barbara Cartland.

Dame Barbara was well in with the Royal family, and one day a letter arrived from Prince Charles inviting Diana and her sisters to a ball at Buckingham Palace.

You are cordially invited to a Ball by Prince Charles

Disco   Late Bar   RSVP

Alas, Diana had no dress to wear so she stayed at home cleaning the hearth while her ugly sister, Lady Jane Fellows, went to the ball and dined with the Prince.

One is a big fan of the Three Degrees

One too

As she swept up cinders Diana dreamt of going to a ball in a golden coach and meeting the handsome Prince.

And deep down inside she knew that one day her dream would come true.

41

Continues on page 48

THE CURSE of DEVIL'S ROCK

TOGETHER WITH HIS WIFE PEGGY, JIM BAXTER WAS SPENDING THE WEEKEND AT HIS UNCLE'S LIGHTHOUSE ON DEVIL'S ROCK, OFF THE COAST OF SCOTLAND

JIM! PEGGY! COME IN!

HELLO UNCLE SILAS - HOW ARE YOU?

NOT SO GOOD, JIM. I - I'VE DECIDED TO LEAVE THE LIGHTHOUSE — FOREVER!

LEAVE? BUT WHY? THIS IS YOUR HOME

THERE IS AN... EVIL PRESENCE HERE, JIM. SINISTER "ACCIDENTS" INVOLVING ITEMS OF UPHOLSTERED FURNITURE HAVE BEEN OCCURRING LATELY

JUST LAST WEEK I BECAME DANGEROUSLY ENTANGLED IN THE DRAYLON SLIP-COVER OF A SCATTER CUSHION ON MY SOFA. I'M AFRAID, JIM - AFRAID FOR MY LIFE!

AYE, YOU MIGHT WELL BE AFRAID, MR SILAS! FOR IT IS THE CURSE...

THE CURSE OF DEVIL'S ROCK!

KABOOM!

OLD MR McTAVISH WAS THE ASSISTANT LIGHTHOUSE KEEPER

EXACTLY ONE HUNDRED YEARS AGO A SHIP CARRYING A CARGO OF SOFT HOUSEHOLD FURNISHINGS CAPSIZED IN THESE WATERS. ALL HANDS WERE LOST

BEFORE HE DROWNED, THE CAPTAIN CURSED DEVIL'S ROCK LIGHTHOUSE, AND SWORE THAT ITS INHABITANTS WOULD HAVE BUT ONE FATE — DEATH BY FURNITURE!

STUFF AND NONSENSE! SURELY YOU DON'T BELIEVE THAT SUPERSTITIOUS RUBBISH, UNCLE

SIT YOURSELF DOWN, AND I'LL MAKE US ALL A NICE CUP OF TEA

BUT SUDDENLY

AHH! I'VE FALLEN THROUGH THE SEAT!

TWANG

AIEEEE!

IT'S UNCLE SILAS! HE'S BROKEN BOTH ARMS AND LEGS, AND SUFFERED MASSIVE INTERNAL INJURIES

BUT WHAT HAPPENED?

IT LOOKS LIKE SOME SUPERNATURAL FORCE HAS CAUSED THE SEAT TO SIMPLY GIVE WAY WHEN UNCLE SILAS SAT ON IT

HE PLUNGED NEARLY TWO INCHES THROUGH THE CHAIR FRAME - AND NEARLY DIED AS A RESULT

I WARNED YE OF THE CURSE! WE MUST LEAVE THIS PLACE, AFORE WE ALL BECOME VICTIMS OF SOME HIDEOUS OCCULT FURNITURE - RELATED CALAMITY!

(COUGH, CHOKE) MR McTAVISH IS RIGHT. WE WILL LEAVE FIRST THING IN THE MORNING

LATE THAT NIGHT

JIM — WHAT ARE YOU DOING?

COME ALONG, PEGGY

WE'RE GOING TO TAKE A CLOSER LOOK AT THE CHAIR THAT ALMOST KILLED UNCLE SILAS!

AND, DOWNSTAIRS

JUST AS I SUSPECTED! IT WASN'T SUPERNATURAL FORCES THAT CAUSED THE SEAT TO COLLAPSE AT ALL!

SEE - THE WEBBING HAS BEEN FIXED TO THE SEAT FRAME WITH LIGHTWEIGHT 10mm TACKS...

BUT EVERY UPHOLSTERER KNOWS THAT, FOR WEBBING WORK, YOU NEED TO USE THE MORE HEAVY DUTY 16mm TACK WITH THE BROADER HEAD, IN ORDER TO SUPPORT THE CONCENTRATION OF WEIGHT DISTRIBUTED OVER THE SEAT AREA

YOU MEAN WHOEVER UPHOLSTERED THIS CHAIR INTENDED IT TO COLLAPSE?

YES — BUT WHO IS THIS DEADLY MENDER OF CHAIRS?

I'LL GIVE YOU ONE GUESS, MY CLEVER FRIEND!

MR McTAVISH!

GUN

SO, YOU WERE MERELY TRYING TO SCARE UNCLE SILAS AWAY FROM THE LIGHTHOUSE; BUT WHY?

SIMPLE! IT WAS MY PLAN TO SOMEHOW OR OTHER TURN THIS LIGHTHOUSE INTO A GREAT BIG SPACE ROCKET AND FLY AROUND THE UNIVERSE IN IT

GUN

I COULD WEAR A SHINY SILVER SPACE-SUIT, AND MY SPACE LIGHTHOUSE WOULD PREVENT OTHER SPACE SHIPS FROM CRASHING INTO ASTEROIDS, AND STUFF

IT'D BE REALLY GREAT!

WELL THIS SHOULD STOP YOU TURNING THE LIGHTHOUSE INTO A BIG SPACE ROCKET AND FLYING AROUND THE UNIVERSE IN IT!

CRACK

UHHH!

NEXT MORNING

...SO THAT STORY OF A CURSE WAS JUST A RUSE TO DRIVE ME AWAY!

THANKS KIDS. HOW CAN I EVER REPAY YOU FOR WHAT YOU'VE DONE?

JUST PROMISE THAT YOU'LL KEEP THE BEACON LIT HERE IN YOUR LONELY WINDSWEPT OUTPOST TO GUARD OVER THOSE IN PERIL ON THE TREACHEROUS SEA, UNCLE SILAS

THAT IS ALL THE REWARD I COULD EVER ASK FOR

ME TOO

42

he's **mr. LOGIC**
HE'LL drive you FRANTIC WITH his PeDANTiC antics

BRMMMMMM!

YES! YELLOW CAR! I NEED ONE FOR ME 147 BREAK!

NER! NER! NER! NER! NER! NER! NER!

STEP OUT OF THE VEHICLE. IS THIS **YOUR** CAR, SIR?
YES.

DO YOU KNOW THE REGISTRATION NUMBER?
YES.

WELL... WHAT IS IT?
IT IS THE MARK BY WHICH THE VEHICLE IS DISTINGUISHED FROM OTHER VEHICLES BY THE DRIVER VEHICLE LISCENSING AUTHORITY, AND MAY THUS BE INDENTIFED BY THE CENTRAL COMPUTER AT SWANSEA.

GEORGE! ASSISTANCE PLEASE. I THINK WE'VE GOT A COMEDIAN.

HOW FAST DO Y'THINK YOU WAS GOIN' THEN?
IF I WAS TO RELY ENTIRELY ON THE ACCURACY OF THE CAR'S SPEEDOMETER, I WOULD SAY THAT I WAS TRAVELLING AT 27 MILES PER HOUR AT THE MOMENT THAT I PASSED YOUR STATIONARY VEHICLE.

WE CLOCKED YOU AT 40 AND 50, YOU WAS TEAR-ARSIN'
YEAH. TONKIN'-ON YOU WAS. 50 AND 60.

NO. IMPOSSIBLE. ALLOW ME TO ELUCIDATE.

I PULLED AWAY FROM THE TRAFFIC LIGHTS—WHICH WE SHALL REFER TO AS 'X'. NOW, MY STARTING VELOCITY WAS 'u' WHICH EQUALS NAUGHT, ACCELERATING AT A RATE OF 'a' METRES PER SECOND SQUARED, TO REACH POINT 'Y' AT TERMINAL VELOCITY 'V' IN TIME 'T'. WE OF COURSE ASSUME CONSTANT ACCELERATION.

10 MINUTES LATER...
...THIS OF COURSE DOES NOT TAKE INTO ACCOUNT THE GEARING RATIOS OF THE VEHICLE, BUT THE ACCURACY WOULD NOT BE AFFECTED BY MORE THAN ONE MILE PER HOUR PLUS OR MINUS 10%. SO, EVEN ASSUMING AN ACCURACY OF 98% FOR THE CO-EFFICIENT OF FRICTION ON A WET SURFACE...

LATER STILL...
...SO, 'V' IS LESS THAN, OR EQUAL TO TWENTY-SEVEN MILES PER HOUR. WELL WITHIN THE SPEED LIMIT.

SHOVE!
SMASH!

HERE. YOUR HEADLIGHT'S BUST.
I HAVE JUST WITNESSED YOU DELIBERATELY BREAK IT WITH YOUR TRUNCHEON FORENSIC TESTS WILL NO DOUBT PROVE THIS.

IT'S AN OFFENCE TO DRIVE A VEHICLE IN THAT STATE.
INDEED. BUT I HAVE A SPARE HEADLIGHT GLASS IN THE GLOVE COMPARTMENT.

RIGHT. I'VE HAD ENOUGH OF THIS. INTO THE BACK O' THE VAN.
HMMM... I FEAR A FAMILIAR SCENARIO IN WHICH I WILL BE SYSTEMATICALLY BEATEN WITHIN THE CONFINES OF THE VEHICLE, OUT OF SIGHT OF THE PUBLIC, AND CONSEQUENTLY MY INJURIES BLAMED ON A FICTITIOUS ACCIDENT INVOLVING A FLIGHT OF STAIRS AT THE POLICE STATION. EVIDENCE WILL BE FALSIFIED TO BACK UP THIS STORY. I WILL SUBSEQUENTLY BE JAILED FOR ASSAULTING A POLICE OFFICER AND RESISTING ARREST.

HERE GEORGE! HE'S SLIPPED DOWN THEM STEPS! HO! HO! HO!
THUMP! BIFF! THUD!

CONSEQUENTLY...
WHACK!
OUCH! FASCINATING... EXACTLY AS I SUMMISED. OOF!

NOW, IF I MAY SUGGEST, SINCE LINES OF STRESS RUN PERPENDICULAR TO THE STRATA IN A SEDIMENTARY ROCK SUCH AS GRANITE, A MORE EFFICIENT METHOD OF FRACTURE WOULD BE TO STRIKE THE ROCK PARALLEL TO THE PLANE OF IT'S WEAKNESS.

ALWAYS STRIKE THE WEAKEST POINT, i.e. HERE.

WHACK!

CRAK! SKRIT! KRACK! KRICK!

hmmm... FASCINATING.

Letterbocks

Good Mourning TV

I READ somewhere that when the Queen Mother (God bless her) eventually passes away the BBC and ITV will cancel all programmes for an official **mourning period of nine days, and broadcast only sombre music and other 'suitable material' as a mark of respect.** Nine days without any decent telly! I suggest your readers start stocking up on videos as quickly as they can. They'll be like gold dust once she pegs it.

**T. O'Shanta
Dundee**

They say that all property is theft. But they also say that possession is nine tenths of the law. Given that you possess all your property, theft is therefore nine tenths of the law. But try telling that to the judge next time you're up for shop lifting.

**H. Mence
HMP Dartmoor**

It's surely one of life's great paradoxes that having 'green fingers' means you are a good gardener, whilst having brown fingers means you can't wipe your arse properly.

**M.H.
Bakewell**

Further to the letter from a Mr O'Shanta (above left). I also heard that if the Queen Mother died during the coming European Football Championships England would withdraw from the competition as a mark of respect. Respect? Personally I don't think allowing the krauts or the frogs to pick up the silverware unchallenged is particularly respectful. We may as well invite them to dance on the old dear's grave whilst waving the trophy in the air.

**D. Stalker
Cambridge**

THIS IS ONE OF OUR MOST POPULAR MODELS MR. GRAYSON. ITS ROUND - ITS ORANGE - AND ITS GUARANTEED RESISTANT TO SEAWATER FOR 10 YEARS.

MMM. SEEMS LIKE A NICE BUOY.

Letterbocks,
P.O. Box 1PT,
Newcastle upon
Tyne, NE99 1PT

I see that do gooder Anita Roddick has converted an office block into emergency housing for the homeless. All well and good, but giving these people somewhere to live will simply create a new problem. Once inside they will cease to be homeless, and immediately they'll have to be evicted to make room for genuinely homeless people still living outside.

This is the real world Mrs Roddick. Solving Britain's homeless problem is a lot harder than making expensive shampoo out of cucumbers.

**B. B. Capp
Kettering**

Greedy Pigs

Its coming to something when schoolchildren are asked to pay £6.50 for a guinea pig - £5.45 more than the advertised price. Pet shops nowadays are simply a law unto themselves.

**Mrs Ann E. Bonnet
Fareham, Hants.**

How about a picture of a bird with no knickers on looking at Berlin through some binoculars, with her arse sticking out?

**Lister & Randall
West Yorkshire**

* Only too happy to oblige lads. What would YOU like to see in Viz? Send your photo requests to our usual address.

Holy unacceptable

As a boozing and over the hill reprobate I have no axe to grind for the Christian establishment, however I did take exception to your piss poor joke on Christ appearing in a pool of vomit (issue 77). Cowardly and disgusting, all in one. I bet you wouldn't do a similar hatchet job on Mohammed. Chances are that if you did at very least you'd get your windows kicked in by a bunch of rabid Moslems. Better still they might call for a Fatwa and have you irreligious bastards killed outright.

**W.E. Walker
Carnforth, Lancs.**

* Calm down Mr Walker. If you get any more 'cross' someone might nail Jesus to you. Geddit?

Please can you tell your readers what you are going to say to your maker on the last day following your most recent religious article (issue 77). You see, we won't be there when you are called to account and somehow I don't think Christ will find you very amusing.
Print this if you dare.

**Ex Viz reader
Yarm, Cleveland**

* Good question, anonymous God botherer of Yarm. What would YOU say to your maker if called to account? Perhaps theologists or Christian readers can come up with some ideas? Write to our usual address, and mark your envelope 'Meet Your Maker'. A tenner for every letter we print.

Bringing home the Bacon

About three years ago you said you'd send a fiver to anyone who spotted a Viz lookalike. Well here's a picture of Mutha Bacon I came across recently. In order to facilitate the above headline I found it at work and *brought it home* this afternoon.

**Dennis Taylor
Chigwell, Essex**

"War! What is it good for?" asked Edwin Starr in his 1970 pop hit. Well Mr Starr, releasing Europe from the grip of a genocidal megalomaniac is one thing that springs to mind.

**P. Pom
Harwich**

Prolapse of Concentration

Next time Uri Geller asks TV viewers at home to put a spoon on top of their TV and concentrate on trying to bend it, instead of concentrating on the spoon lets all concentrate on Uri prolapsing and see what happens.

**Simone Glover
Tottenham**

My father always believed that laughter was the best form of medicine. Perhaps that's why so many of our family died from tuberculosis.

**J. Thanin
St Ratford**

e's got a ne-apple, his hand

se find enclosed a ...ure of Tony Hadley (... of Spandau Ballet) ...g presented with his ... own 'Gold' Pine-...le in the light of your ...rtisement (issue 77). ...cut a long story short ...y, now 62 and very ...ch an *old* romantic, is ...rently starring as ...ager Johnny Malone ...hugga Looga Baby, a ...en homage to the ...es teen movies being ...le for the Fuji Film ...ards to be held at ...FTA later this year. ...haps in years to come ...y, who still always ...eves in his soul, will be ...pping his gold pine-...le for an Oscar.

Kate Vale
Ah-huh-huh Films
Sheffield

Popular singer turned actor Mr. Tony Hadley (right), out of Spandau Ballet, is pleased to receive a Gold pineapple off some bloke in Sheffield yesterday.

Jet disaster

My nomination for the unluckiest man in the world must surely be Jet Harris out of The Shadows. Once in his entire lifetime Sir Cliff Richard shags a bird, and who does he choose? Poor old Jet's missus. Perhaps any mathematicians among your readers could tell us what the odds of that happening were. I wish I'd had a fiver on it, that's for sure.

A. Capp
Rochdale

My Fave Dictator
Number 51
STING

" *I admire Napoleon ...nd the way he ...nvented metric and ...ried to conquer ...Russia in the olden ...days when it was ...nowing.* "

...ext week: Ted Nugent ...alks about Hitler.

FISHERMEN. A dead rabbit makes an ideal 'grow bag' for maggots.
Pam Anahat
Huddersfield

DIRTY carpets? Make your own 'Hoover' by fixing door draft excluder brushes to the blades of an old petrol lawn mower.
Sam Brairo
Truro

GIVE your clothes that 'Elvis sparkle' by allowing a snail to crawl all over you.
J. Elvis
Jarrow

CHEFS. When fixing together the pieces of a broken cake dry pasta spirals make perfect 'screws'.
JT
Morpeth

OFFICE workers. Top up that fading holiday tan during quiet moments by lying naked on the photocopier and pressing the 'copy' button.
Mark Anderson
West Hampstead

OLD FOLK. Keep your living room warm in winter by plugging in your electric iron and using it as a door stop.
Michael Harby
Bakewell

CLAUSTROPHOBICS. Reduce the risk of panic when entering a lift by looking through the wrong end of a pair of binoculars.
T. R. Ilbey
Hattington

HEELS from an old pair of shoes are the ideal shape for blocking up mouse holes in your skirting board.
Tom Boler
Brimsford

GIVE yourself an 'Elvis style' lip by knotting a piece of cotton thread and lodging it between your two front teeth, pulling it tight and then wrapping the other end several times around your ear.
B. Idol
Hospital, Hollywood

GENTS. After visiting the barber remove hairs from the back of your neck by inflating a balloon, rubbing it on your jumper in order to charge it with static electricity, and then gently brushing it along the collar line and around your ears.
B. Derby-Hatt
Luton

AGROPHOBICS. Feel more comfortable in large open spaces by looking the right way through a pair of binoculars.
T. R. Ilbey
Hattington

GIVE your pet tortoise protective 'bull bars' by slipping the wire off a champagne cork over his head.
J. Bobble
Tinsley

RESTRING that old tennis racket with piano wire. Hey presto! A "chipper" for potatoes, carrots, boiled eggs etc. which also allows you to practice your serve whilst cooking.
John Tait
Thropton

AMAZE your neighbours by tight rope walking across your clothes line without the use of a safety net. Simply thread the clothes line through short sections of hosepipe glued to the bottom of your shoes. Providing your shoe laces are tied tightly, falling off is impossible.
M. Board
Romney

CONVERT any old hat to a smart 'Sherlock Holmes' style deer stalker by draping a pair of socks down over your ears before donning the hat. Remember to catch the socks when your hat is doffed.
Robert Stetson
Jedburgh

STEEL wool moistened with a drop of oil is ideal for wiping baby robots bottoms with.
JT
Northumberland

CAN YOU LEND ME TEN QUID TILL I GET ME GIRO?

DOCTOR. IT'S MY LEG. I THINK IT'S BROKE.

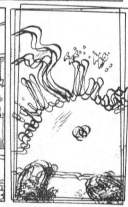

46

John sucks tramps cocks.
100%. True.

47

Continued from page 41

DIANA: PRINCESS OF HEARTS

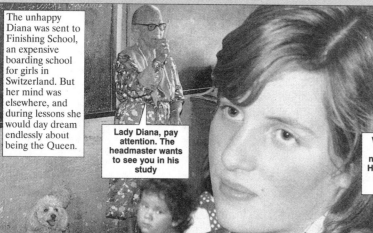

The unhappy Diana was sent to Finishing School, an expensive boarding school for girls in Switzerland. But her mind was elsewhere, and during lessons she would day dream endlessly about being the Queen.

Lady Diana, pay attention. The headmaster wants to see you in his study

These exam results are dreadful. What career did you have in mind, Miss Diana?

I want to be the Queen, sir.

Well, two GCSEs simply isn't good enough. You need at least five for that. Have you ever considered being a nanny for posh kids?

With her poncy background Diana was ideally suited to being a nanny for toff children. But her heart was never in the job. One day in the kinder garden...

Ay hate being a nenny for torffs. Ay'd rather be the Queen. The Queen of England.

Nenny, may we hev some bread to feed the dacks?

You may hev a slep round the frigging lughole if you don't shat your bleedin' mouths!

Meanwhile at Buckingham Palace the Queen has summonded Prince Charles to see her.

Charles, if you don't get married soon people will think you're a shirt lifter

What about that chubby actress you were seeing? The one out of Straw Dogs

I liked her mum, but she's not a virgin. Not by a long chalk. What with the sixties and everything there's not many virgins left nowadays

That evening the Queen looked into her magic mirror.

Mirror mirror on the wall, is there any virgins left at all?

The magic mirror spoke...

"There is but one who's worth a try, a posh nann-ny called Lady Di. She's probably your son's best bet, Cos' no-one's popped her cherry yet."

And in the mirror Diana's face appeared.

Ha ha ha! At long last I've found her. Bring the virgin to me!

Continues on page 56

SPOILT BASTARD

Panel 1: AT SCHOOL... I'M SORRY TO CALL YOU IN **AGAIN**, MRS. TIMPSON, BUT TIMMY'S BEHAVIOUR HAS GOT **MUCH** WORSE SINCE WE LAST MET

OH, DEAR. I'M SURE IT ISN'T HIS FAULT, HEADMASTER

HEADMASTER

TICK TICK TICKETY

TICK TICK TICK TICK TICKETY TICK TICK

Panel 2: WELL, I'M AFRAID BITING IS SOMETHING WE CAN'T ALLOW, AS I'M SURE YOU'LL UNDERSTAND. HE HAS NOW BITTEN EVERYONE IN THE SCHOOL AT LEAST ONCE. I'VE HAD PARENTS QUEUING UP TO COMPLAIN...TWO OF THE DINNER LADIES HAVE REFUSED TO GO NEAR HIM...

MR. THOM

Panel 3: HE BIT GINGER JOHNSON ON THE ARM AND FETCHED BLOOD, AND FATTY ATKINSON NEARLY LOST AN EAR YESTERDAY

WELL, HE MUST HAVE BEEN PROVOKED. MY TIMMY DOESN'T BITE FOR NO REASON

Panel 4: WELL, I'M SORRY, MRS. TIMPSON, BUT I'M GOING TO HAVE TO EXCLUDE HIM FROM SCHOOL FOR TEN DAYS...

OH, DEAR, BUT...

...AND I'VE ARRANGED FOR HIM TO SEE AN EDUCATIONAL PSYCHOLOGIST

Panel 5: OUCH! EH!?!

Panel 6: WHAT'S GOING ON? HE BIT ME, MR. THOM, HERE...ON MY ARM...LOOK...HE'S LEFT **TEETH MARKS**

Panel 7: OH, TIMMY, WHY DID YOU BITE MISS SIMM? SHE TOLD ME TO TAKE MY HANDS OUT OF THE FISH TANK. I ONLY WANTED TO TAKE A FISH OUT AND SQUASH IT. THERE'S HUNDREDS OF THEM IN THERE...

...SHE TRIED TO PULL ME AWAY SO I BIT HER!

Panel 8: OH, I'M SURE SHE DIDN'T MEAN IT, TIMMY...COME ON, WE'LL TELL HER SHE UPSET YOU AND SHE'LL APOLOGISE

! GASP!

Panel 9: SHORTLY...

FULCHESTER SOCIAL SERVICE DEPT. OF CHILD PSYCHOLOGY

Panel 10: HI, NICE TO MEET YOU, MRS. TIMPSON. I'M WILFY WICHARDSON. NICE TO MEET YOU. CALL ME WILFY...

HEY, YOU MUST BE TIMMY. GWEAT! CAN I CALL YOU TIM? NO!

WILF WICHARDSON CHILD PSYCHOLOGIST

Panel 11: MAKE YOURSELF AT HOME, AND I'LL EXPWAIN WHAT I'M GOING TO DO...I'M GOING TO FIND OUT...**WHY**...TIM IS EXHIBITATALIZING DYSFUNCTIONAL-ISTIC BEHAVIOURISMS

OH...ER...THAT'S NICE YEH!

Panel 12: GOT ONE! HEY, TIM...YOU'VE CAUGHT A FISH...**GWEAT**...

...TELL YOU WHAT. PUT THE LITTLE FELLOW BACK AND WE'LL...

Panel 13: SQUASHED IT! HA!

LOB! SPLATCH!

Panel 14: HMM! HE'S PWOJECTIONALISING HIS ANGER...IF YOU WILL...ONTO THE FISH. THAT'S GOOD. **VEWWY** GOOD...YOU SEE... QUITE FWEQUENTIONALISTICALLY, THIS BEHAVIOUR STEMS FWOM LOW SELF ESTEEM. TIM FEELS...IN A SENSE...INADEQUATE

YES...YES, I **DO**

WE MUST TWY TO EMPATHISALISE WITH THAT LACK OF EMPOWERMENT.

Panel 15: ...BEHAVIOUR LIKE THIS IS OFTEN TWIGGERED BY SOME EVENT AT HOME...

THERE! SEE! IT'S **YOUR** FAULT. YOU'VE TWISTED ME AND NOW I'M MENTAL. I'M NOT TO BLAME FOR ANY OF MY BEHAVIOUR. **YOU ARE!**

Panel 16: HEY, TIM...NO! YOU'RE NOT MENTAL **OR** BADLY BEHAVED. YOU NEED SOME POSITIVE FEEDBACK...IT'S NOT DIFFICULT. WE CAN TEACH YOU WEELAXATION TECHNIQUES...BUILD UP YOUR CONFIDENCE WITH WOLE PLAY WORKSHOPS AND GWOUP HUGGING SESSIONS...

...BE POSITIVE!

Panel 17: SO... WIGHT THEN, TIM, LET'S START...TELL ME WHAT YOU **LIKE** DOING? WHAT ARE YOU **GOOD** AT?

BITING PEOPLE...AND SQUASHING FISH, YOU BEARDY WEIRDY

ERM...GOOD, GOOD, YEH! THAT'S GOOD

Panel 18: ER...LOOK, MRS. TIMPSON, I THINK TIM'S PROBLEMS ARE A LITTLE MORE COMPLEXATIONAL THAN I FIRST THOUGHT

OH, I KNOW. I'VE TRIED EVERYTHING. I'VE HALVED HIS SMARTIES RATION, STOPPED HIM WATCHING HORROR VIDEOS AFTER THREE IN THE MORNING...

...I EVEN ONCE THOUGHT ABOUT SLAPPING HIS LEGS

Panel 19: **HEY, WOAH!...NO!**..NEVER VIOLENCE, MRS. TIMPSON. VIOLENCE IS A, LIKE, BAD SCENE. CHASTISEMENTISATIONAL ABUSE WON'T SOLVE TIM'S PWOBLEM...

Panel 20: ...ONE HAS TO LOOK ON DIFFICULT KIDS AS...PEOPLE...TALK TO THEM...WIN THEIR CONFIDENCE ABOVE ALL, LISTEN TO THEM.

YOU GO TO THE CANTEEN AND HAVE A DWINK OF TEA...

...LEAVE ME TO GET TO KNOW TIM

Panel 21: WIGHT, TIM...LET'S ME AND YOU HAVE A LITTLE CHAT, EH?

Y'KNOW, I THINK WE'RE GOING TO BE GWEAT FWIENDS

Panel 22: AN HOUR LATER...

I'LL JUST SEE HOW THEY'RE GETTING ON

WILF RICHARDSON CHILD PSYCHOLOGIST

Panel 23: BITE ME WOULD YOU, Y'LITTLE FUCKIN' BASTARD. I'LL TAKE THE FUCKIN SKIN OFF YER ARSE. I'M SURPRISED YOUR MOTHER HASN'T KILLED YOU Y'LITTLE...FUCKIN'..FUCK...

WHACK! WHACK! WHACKITY WHACK!

WHAAAAAAAAAAAH!

Future goes back to the future

THE year by which time scientists predict new and unproven inventions are expected to be in everyday use is set to change.

For decades 2000 has been the official scientific 'Year of the Future'. Throughout the years boffins have confidently predicted that all manner of new ideas and inventions - from battery powered cars to holographic TVs - will be in common use 'by the year 2000'. But as the end of the millennium dawns, science chiefs from around the world have met in secret to agree to a postponement of the deadline.

Butlers

Red faced researchers are thought to have realised within the last two years that predictions such as robot butlers, aluminium foil clothing, cars that drive themselves, small tablets entirely replacing food and dome shaped silver houses would not be available by the due date of 2000 due to teething technological problems. And after a meeting of the world's leading scientists in Geneva earlier this month a new date has now officially been set - the year 2020.

Stans

Professor Anthony Ockenden, chairman of the 40 strong panel of scientists who gathered from around the world to agree the new year, explained what their decision actually meant .

Boffins' 20-20 vision of things to come

"Quite simply, any far fetched futuristic invention conceived from this date onwards should be in the shops by the year 2020. Any invention which has failed to meet the old deadline of 2000 will be carried over to the new one."

Blakeys

Today's news comes as a bitter blow to householders hoping to find space age solutions to everyday problems. Irene Gubbins of Ebchester had been looking forward to a holiday on the Moon which she had been lead to believe would be possible by the year 2000. Now she faces the prospect of another twenty year wait. "It's diabolical. What do I tell my kids? They've been looking forward to it ever since they heard James Burke talk about it on telly in the sixties. I promised them wrist watch TVs as well. This is a bloody disgrace".

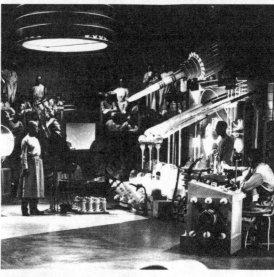

Meanwhile presenters of BBC's Tomorrow's World were delighted. One former host, ageing leggy soapdish TV brainbox Carol Vauderman, described it as a 'great relief'. "As the millennium approached some of our predictions were looking more and more dodgy. Today's announcement is a lifeline. It will keep the show going another 20 years at least."

Carol Vorderman shows us the future (left) and (above) the future as it would appear in the Year 2000, yesterday.

Childrens TV presenters were equally pleased. Blue Peter, which was due to be presented by robots by the year 2000, immediately announced plans to bury a box in the Blue Peter Garden for the year 2020. Presenters Diane Jordan was delighted. "It will contain, amongst other things a newspaper, photographs of the presenters and their pets and film footage of us digging up the Blue Peter box for the year 2000".

COCKNEY WANKER

ORWIGHT DARLIN'

WANKER'S MOTORS
QUALITY USED CARS — RAC INSPECTED

CAN'T SEE THE CAR YOU WANT? JUST ASK, AND WE'LL GET ONE

1 LADY OWNER

RUNS SMASHIN

CHOICE OF LOG BOOKS

CAR OF THE WEEK £8000

ALL OUR CARS GUARANTEED FOREVER!

CASH PAID FOR STOLEN CARS & RINGERS

INSURANCE WRITE OFFS BOUGHT FOR CASH

YEAH... ONLY TWO 'UNDRED AN' FIFTY MILES ON THE CLOCK... BELONGED TO A NUN, THIS ONE... COULDN'T DRIVE... KEPT IT IN THE GARAGE SHE DID

CAR OF THE WEEK £8000

BUT THE FRONT'S A RED ESCORT AND THE BACK'S A BLUE ANGLIA

YEAH! NICE, INNIT. THAT'S YER ACTUAL TWO TONE, THAT IS, CHIEF! HIGHLY SOUGHT ARFTER, THEY ARE. AN' I'LL NOT CHARGE YER NO EXTRA FOR IT, I WON'T

I'M NOT SURE... EIGHT THOUSAND IS A LOT OF MONEY FOR A 'P' REG

WELL YEH! BUT THE FRONT'S A 'W'

HMM! I'LL HAVE A THINK ABOUT IT

WELL I WOULDN'T FINK ABAAT IT TOO LONG, JOHN. I 'AD SAMBODY LOOKIN' AT IT THIS MORNIN'...

IN FACT, HE'S CAMIN' BACK WIN THE CASH...

CAR OF WEEK £8000

OFFERED NINE GWAND FOR IT. HE'LL BE 'ERE IN FIVE MINUTES. BUT I'LL TELL YER WOT.... I LIKE YOU, SQUIRE. THAT SMILE ON YOUR FACE IS WORF A GWAND TO ME... I'LL LETCHA 'AVE IT F' TEN

ERM... I'LL HAVE TO SPEAK TO MY WIFE

OH! 'ERE HE CAMS... HE'S GOT THE CASH WIV' 'IM, D'Y' WANT IT OR DONTCHA?

ER

MAKE YER MIND AP. HE'LL BE 'ERE IN FIFTEEN SECONDS...

...TEN...NINE...EIGHT...SEVEN...

ER...COULD I BORROW YOUR PHONE TO CALL MY WIFE?

NO...FIVE...FOUR...FWEE...TWO...

ALRIGHT... **SOLD!** I'LL HAVE IT!

LAVERLY JABERLY. THAT'LL BE TEN GWAND...

...CASH!

SO...

THANKS. OH... CAN I HAVE THE LOG BOOK, PLEASE?

THERE YOU GO, ME OLD CHINA. 'APPY MOTORIN'

LOG BOOK?... OH, I POSTED THAT TO YER YESTERDAY... YOU SHOULD GEDDIT IN THE MORNIN'

OH, GREAT... AND WHAT ABOUT THE GUARANTEE?

GUARANTEE!?

...GUARANTEE?... THAT SIGN IS THE ONLY GUARANTEE YOU NEED, JOHN. A LIFETIMES COMMITMENT TO MY CASTOMERS THAT'S WOT THAT IS

ANY PROBLEMS YOU CAM BACK TO ME...

KER'S MOTORS
ALITY USED CARS

...I CAN'T SAY FAIRER THAN THAT, CAN I? LISTEN, I'LL EVEN TOP THE GEARBOX AP FOR YA BEFORE YER GO... MAKE A NICE SMOOVE RIDE

THAT'S VERY NICE OF YOU

...'ANDSOM!

PLEVIN'S MULTIGRADE SAWDUST

VROOOM! VROOOM!

VROOOM! VROOOM!

SNAP!!

WANKER'S MOTORS
QUAL TY

ARFTERNOON, SQUIRE! WOT CAN I DO FOR YOU, THEN?

I'M SORRY TO BOTHER YOU, BUT THE CAR I'VE JUST BOUGHT OFF YOU HAS JUST... WELL... IT'S FALLEN TO BITS!

CAR! WOT CAR? I NEVER SOLD YOU A CAR... I AIN'T NEVER SEEN YOU BEFORE IN MY WHOLE LIFE!

THAT CAR. I'VE JUST GIVE YOU TEN GRAND FOR IT TEN SECONDS AGO... REMEMBER?

YOU PAID TEN GWAND FOR **THIS!?** YOU MAST BE A FACKIN' NATTAH! DEAR OH DEAR

IT'S A BLADDY WRECK, INNIT?

TELL YER WOT... I'LL GIVE YER TWENTY QUID F' SCRAP...

...AN' I'M TAKIN A BIG RISK 'COS I DON'T KNOW YOU FWOM ADAM

BUT...I...

ALWIGHT THEN, FIFTEEN, AN' THAT'S ME FINAL OFFER...

BUT I'VE JUST PAI...

FOURTEEN...FIRTEEN... TWELVE...ELEVEN...

ALRIGHT! I'LL TAKE IT

KER'S MOTORS
USED CARS

CAR OF THE WEEK £12000

CUTS AND SHOTS BOUGHT

GPD ST CD 5-95

VIZ 78

51

Clowns see red over circus tax

CIRCUS clowns are paying through their red noses for big shoes as a result of Britain's barmy tax laws.

So says Tory MP Winston Churchill whose grandfather won the war.

Shoes

Under present rules children's shoes - sizes five and under - are exempt from VAT. However young clowns who wear big shoes as a vital part of their job are being forced to pay the extra tax when they buy adult size shoes.

Brass

Yet the bizarre tax laws are a boon for adult circus dwarfs, most of whom only wear children's sizes. The average circus dwarf can save up to £75 a year on unpaid VAT by wearing shoes that are size five or under.

Hooves

"The situation is a non-sense", claims Mr Churchill who is a long time campaigner on behalf of circus clowns. "I believe this minority of people are receiving unfair treatment under existing UK tax legislation. When you consider that the average clown is probably spending hundreds of pounds a year on dry cleaning to get custard off his clothes, and fish out of his pants, to make him pay extra for his shoes is totally unfair."

Box

Mr Churchill spoke as a convoy of clowns arrived at Westminster yesterday

VAT'll not do nicely on big shoes

Slapstick MP Churchill (left) and a hard hit clown with comedy shoes (above).

to protest about new MOT regulations which they claim are also discriminatory. Their convoy of cars left Brighton in February of last year and took almost 16 months to complete the journey due to their doors falling off and the engines blowing up all the time. "These new regulations are a tax on comedy motorists and will place hundreds of livelihoods at risk", said the MP yesterday.

Mr Churchill comes from a traditional circus background. His father was a high wire monocyclist and Mr Churchill himself is a lion tamer at weekends. Chancellor of the Exchequer Mr. Kenneth Clark, who has vowed to review the clown tax situation in his next budget, is himself a keen amateur bare back horse rider and escapologist.

TRAVELLING THROUGH SPACE AND TIME TRYING TO FIND SOMEWHERE TO HAVE A BIG SHIT

QUICK! HURRY DOCTOR! THEY'RE GAINING ON YE!

DID YE MANAGE TAE DROP IT DOCTOR?

DID I FUCK. I HAD ME SHREDDIES DOWN, AND I WAS ACHIN' TO CURL ONE DOWN. NEXT THING I KNEW THESE BLOODY CYBERMEN'S COMIN' AFTER ME!

SET THE CO-ORDINATES FOR ANYWHERE IN SPACE WITH PLENTY OF BUSHES JAMIE. NO ICE PLANETS MIND.

GRIND! CROAK!

QUACK! BRAP!

I THINK WE'VE FOUND A QUIET SPOT DOCTOR. NO APPARENT LIFE FORMS. OXYGEN AT 20%

FUCK THAT! LET ME OUT. I'VE GOT A BROWN TROUT TO DROP!

GET IN! NO-ONE FOR BLOODY MILES!

OOAAH! THIS IS GOING TO BE FABULOUS. IT'S IN THE BOMB-BAY... HERE WE GO...

DOCTOR! LOOK OOT! BEHIND YE!

SEA DEVILS!

AW, BLOODY HELL! ALL OF TIME AND SPACE AT MY FINGERTIPS AND I CAN'T FIND ANYWHERE TO DROP ME FUDGE!

RIGHT JAMIE! I'VE JUST REMEMBERED THERE'S A TOP-NOTCH LITTLE KLUDGEE ON METEBELIS 3. QUICK! SET THE CO-ORDINATES, I'VE GOT THE TURTLES HEAD!

BRAAAP!

HURRY UP, FOR FUCK'S SAKE! I THINK I'M TOUCHING CLOTH!

PARP! TOOT!

GRIND! CROAK!

THE MASTER! FUCK! WHAT ARE YOU DOING IN THERE?

SORRY DOCTOR. BUT I WAS OUT ON THE POP LAST NIGHT ON XERAPHAS. GOT THE SQUIRTS SOMETHING ROTTEN. I THINK I'LL BE IN HERE ALL DAY.

BASTARDS!

OOOH MY POOR RINGPIECE!

SKLUDOOSH!

PARP!

RIGHT! SET THE CO-ORDINATES! ANYWHERE! I AM ABSOLOUTELY FUCKING DESPERATE! WE'VE GOT TO FIND SOMEWHERE RIGHT NOW OR I'LL SHIT MY BLOODY PANTS! I'M CHEWING A FUCKIN' BRICK!

RIGHT DOCTOR!

SO... OKAY. HERE WE ARE DOCTOR. WHERE?

THE PLANET SKARO!

WELL FUCKING DONE! IT'S ONLY THE PLANET OF THE FUCKING DALEKS! BUT SHAG THAT, I NEED A SHIT BIG-TIME! OPEN THOSE DOORS BEFORE I LAY A STONE OF DOG'S EGGS IN ME STRIDES!

HALT! HALT!

PARP! HONK!

INTRUDER!... INTRUDER!... HEADING FOR... DAVROS'S PRIVATE... SHITEHOUSE!... INTRUDER!... INTRUDER!...

SKLUDINK! PLOP-PLOP-PLOP PLOPPETTY-PLOP! PLINK! PLINK!

OOOH! Y'BASTARDS! NECTAR! OOOAH! I FUCKIN' NEEDED THAT! JEESUS!

ZAP!

CHRIST... WHAT... A... STINK! ...CHRIST... WHAT... A... STINK!... CHRIST... WHAT... A... STINK!

DISGUSTING!... DISGUSTING!... DISGUSTING!

YOU... FILTHY... BASTARD!... YOU... FILTHY... BASTARD!... YOU... FILTHY... BASTARD!

HAS... ANYONE... GOT... A... MATCH?

SORRY DAVROS. I'D GIVE IT TEN MINUTES IF I WAS YOU.

NEXT WEEK: THE SONTARANS ATTACK WHILST THE DOCTOR LAYS A CABLE IN A LAYBY OFF THE M6!

Victorian Dad

54

Continued from page 48

One day Di was out walking in Regents Park...

Hey! Aren't you Prince Charles?

I might be. Who's asking?

I'm Di. Lady Di.

I'm Charles, but you can call me Sir.

Listen, I'm starving. Fancy a pizza?

Diana thought she was dreaming as the handsome Prince treated her to a slap up meal. They got on really well, and after they'd finished their pudding Charles called over a violinist.

What's your favourite tune Diana? I'll have him play it for you.

Anything by Duran Duran. How about 'The Reflex'? That's my favourite.

Yeah. Nice one. I'm a bit of a Duranie myself. I like Phil Collins too. He's my favourite solo artist. Who's yours?

Soon it was announced that Charles and Di were to wed.

And finally some good news. At long last Prince Charles is getting married.

The lucky lady is a posh nanny, Princess Diana, who's a virgin. The wedding will be a St Paul's tomorrow morning.

There's something about that Camellia Parker-Knowles I don't like.

At last the big day arrived and Diana, in a dress designed by Mike Oldfield, married her Prince Charming. But as they posed for photographs on the church lawn, one guest seemed unusually familiar with Charles.

Mother. Where's daddy?

Daddy's on holiday in Scotland again, shooting grouses and talking to the trees.

Corrrr! One loves this!!

Diana gave the future King a beautiful young son, William, to be hair to his throne. And with the birth of a second son, Harold, their Royal Family was complete.

The Princess and her two young boys were happy at their new country house, Alton Towers. But Prince Charles was rarely at home.

56

The story continues on page 65

Letterbocks

Judge for yourself

Fan-static idea

❏ **WHY oh why do boffins waste so much money building giant windmill farms and researching wave power?** Surely the most obvious form of alternative energy is static electricity. I calculate that a Zeppelin balloon rubbed on a jumper the size of Wembley Stadium would generate enough electricity to run a town the size of Macclesfield for three weeks. During periods of low demand the energy could be stored by sticking the giant Zeppelins to a wall. It would be a lot safer than nuclear power too. A 'Chernobyl style' disaster at a static electricity power station would at worst consist of a loud 'bang', and result in everyone's hair standing on end for a little bit.

**Professor Ian Fells
Department of Energy
Conversion
University of Newcastle**

P.S. This would also create jobs, as unemployed people could knit the jumpers.

Doc's cock

❏ Here's a picture I took alongside Highway 2 in Northern Michigan, USA. Having wasted my entire career carrying out important medical research, it would at last make my life worthwhile if you were to publish this letter.
**Dr Jeffrey Haudel
Romsey, Hants.**

The aphorism 'clothes maketh man' is incorrect. Any dolt knows that man maketh clothes, or rather, third world women do, in pretty deplorable working conditions.

**T. Foster
Alton, Hants.**

Letterbocks
P.O. Box 1PT
Newcastle upon Tyne
NE99 1PT

❏ Can somebody tell me why Lesley Joseph (Dorian off Birds of a Feather) thinks she's so irresistible to men, as depicted in the Somerfield's TV ads? She's a dog. Now that Samatha Janus on the other hand, I'd crawl through a barrel of broken glass just to stick matches in her shit.

**Andy Dewhurst
Blackpool**

Not so grand pricks

❏ I've just watched the Spanish Grand Prix and can't help thinking what a waste of money such an event is. Why don't those F1 ring nuggets buy a packet of digestives and hold a world series to see who can squirt their curd first. We'd all get to see how small Schumacher's cock is, and the millions saved could feed and clothe the starving in the world.

**Dom Gallimore
Crewe**

❏ If the Government want to ban "dangerous herbs" they could start with parsley. I nearly choked on a sprig of parsley once.

**Dean Mitchell
Stafford**

❏ I'm too drunk to get out of my chair, but I'd like to go to bed. Would any of your readers care to help me up the stairs?

**J. T.
Northampton**

❏ I've been sitting here thinking. It's a good job your blood isn't fizzy, like lemonade. If it was, and you went for a run, you might explode. Or your head could suddenly 'pop' off, like a cork.

**Dr. Jonathon Miller
Royal Opera House
London**

Cliff Richard The Third

❏ In the play 'Macbeth' three witches first predicted that Macbeth would become Thane of Cawdor, which he did. They then predicted he would become King of Scotland, which in due course he did. In issue 47 of Viz (April 1991) Miss Martha Hienkel of Weighbridge suggested that Cliff Richard should be honoured with a Knighthood.

This prophecy came true. She then went on to say it would be nice if Cliff married Princess Ann and became King of England. Need I say more?
Perhaps the first thing Sir Cliff should do when he becomes King is have Mrs Martha Hienkel burnt at the stake as she is clearly a witch. (And perhaps replace the national anthem with his little known 1964 hit 'I could easily fall' which is much nicer than some of his better known recordings.)

**William Langmead
Watford, Herts.**

Ravey Davey GRAVE-y

❏ A few years ago a dopey sod came to work as a grave digger at our cemetery. He was so daft looking we took this picture of him. Doesn't he bear a remarkable resemblance to the Viz character Ravey Davey Gravy?

**Robert Mead
Maidstone, Kent**

P.S. I'm not dead. I work in the cemetery as well.

Paper tissue of lies

❏ A wise man once told me 'don't believe everything you read in the papers'. I've always followed that advice, but I only buy the papers for the TV listings, and consequently I tend to miss an awful lot of my favourite programmes.

**H. Rug
Battersea**

❏ It recently dawned on me what a realistic programme 'The A Team' was. Why, only the other day myself and three friends, jailed for a crime we did not commit, escaped from a high security prison and set about building home made tanks and missiles to fight mini-wars in the streets for no apparent reason, whilst keeping a low profile to avoid the Military Police.

**John McDermott
Smoggieborough**

In reply to the smug Godbotherer of Y (issue 78), when 'called account' on Judgment I will beg God not to m me spend eternity smug, self satisf humourless, guilt rid Jesus freaks who, ou cowardice, weakness fear, live their l according to a hotchpo of old Jewish folk tales try to tell us what is fu while wandering ro with their jumpers tuc into their trousers.

**D. Edwa
Great Yarm**

❏ Further to the let from W.E.Walker and Viz reader of Yarm (is 78). What a pair of tw eh? If Christ really give a shit about you ing the piss out of h case disciples who v alise him in every un surface they encour then he's more o wanker than those two

**Tris Harvey-
Chipping No**

❏ Fuck me, the prev correspondent sound bit posh, doesn't Anyway, on the subje God, the other day w shopping in town I sa vicar carrying an umbr yet it didn't rain at all day. If God really exis surely he would tip vicars when it wasn't g to rain, rather allowing them to c umbrellas round all needlessly. To my n this proves beyond reasonable doubt God doesn't exist.

**Mr F. Carpe
Harley-Davi**

❏ W. E. Walker (issue is talking out his arse w he suggests that you w never dare do a sin spoof on the Islamic f It is a well known fact Islam forbids the re sentation of the hu form in art, so even i face of the Pro Mohammed were appear in a pool of vo nobody would recogn because no-one has faintest idea what looked like. In the lig this astute observa surely I win £5?

**A. Ba
Fai**

I've heard of the 'turtles ad', but this is ridiculous. Do I get a fiver?

Leslie Butler
Lerwick

Robocon

Any readers who are approached in the street by robot tramps asking for money, be warned. Rather than using it to buy nuts and bolts, as often as not these vagrant robots waste the money on cheap oil.

M. Griffiths
Walton

They say that time waits for no man. How prophetic! I went to see the musical 'Time' produced by Dave Clark and starring Laurence Olivier at the Dominion Theatre, London, only to be told that the production had finished over eight years ago.

Julian Morgan
Streatham SW16

Hare conditioner

❏ The other day I gave my pet rabbit a bath using Body Shop shampoo and I was horrified to see its eyes go red and swell like golf balls. If Body Shop had had the sense to test their products on laboratory animals like everyone else, my rabbit would have been saved a considerable amount of discomfort.

W. Weave
Gillingham

Electric sys-tern

❏ Plumbers and electricians must be laughing all the way to the bank. We are being conned, having to have two completely separate systems in our houses. If you stop for a moment and think about it, there's no reason why hot and cold water pipes shouldn't double up as the electrical supply. Live in the hot pipe, neutral in the cold. Waste pipes can be connected to the earth if desired. Electric sockets could then be soldered onto central heating pipes or radiators, with no ugly wiring to conceal.
The system would be perfectly safe, providing you wore rubber gloves and Wellington boots when turning on taps and radiators.

Lionel O'Tiles
Frodingham

CATCH a condor by simply building a wooden stockade 1 metre high and 50 metres in diameter, and then placing a dead goat in the centre. The bird will land inside the stockade to feed on the goat, but will then be unable to get out. This is because condors require a 'run up' of at least 100 metres before they can gain the momentum necessary for take off.

G. Hill
Birmingham

MAKE rowing a boat easier by drilling a few large holes through the oars.

John Tait
Thropton

PROMISE to ring people at specific times, then don't. They'll ring you to see what's wrong, at which point you can have your original planned conversation at their expense.

Dawn Ralphson
Euxton, Lancs.

LAMB for dinner tonight and you've forgotten the mint sauce? No worries. Toothpaste mixed with a little vinegar and chopped nettle leaves makes an ideal emergency replacement.

J.T.
Thropton

OLD FOLK. Make mealtimes easier by employing a set of novelty clockwork teeth to 'pre-chew' your food before it enters your mouth.

J.T.
Thropton

WHEN standing on a chair to change a light bulb always put the chair in position, below the light, before standing on it. It becomes much harder to move the chair once you are standing on it.

T. Macroadstone
Derby

JOY RIDERS. Lie in the freezer all day before going out at nights to steal cars. Then, when you ditch the motor and make a run for it through people's back gardens, you'll be invisible to the thermal imaging cameras on the police helicopter.

Urinal Dockrat
Marsworth, Bucks.

CATCH a monkey by drilling a hole in a hollow tree just wide enough for a monkey's hand to pass through, then put nuts inside the hole. The monkey will stick his hand inside the tree to reach them, but with the nuts in his grasp his hand will be too wide to remove from the hole. The animal will not have the intelligence to drop the nuts in order to effect his escape.

G. Hill
Birmingham

DIFFUSE 'road rage' stand-offs by out stretching your arms and suggesting that you both hug.

Austin Fisher
Finsbury Park N4

ACQUIRE the coolest garden in your street by placing Rayban sunglasses on your gnomes and replacing their fishing rods with small toy shotguns.

N. Aitchison
Nicosia, Cyprus

GIRLS. Stuff a pitta bread with tampons, lipstick, etc. Your friends be green with envy at your 'Vivienne Westwood' style clutch bag.

Bunny McMahon
Cork

POLO mints make excellent 'spearmint washers' for drinking water taps, and after a drink of water they leave your breath minty fresh.

Ramindar Plinth
Ilford

TRY using Cola cubes instead of Oxo cubes. Not only will it put the fizz back into tired old recipes, it also considerably reduces the risk of BSE.

Daisy Duke
Hazzard

SUCK the eyes from attacking zombies using a Black & Decker 'Dustbuster'. The zombies will then wander aimlessly and can be dispatched by the usual methods at a more leisurely pace.

J.T.
Thropton

The MODERN PARENTS

The story so far: Embarrassed by Cressida's new profession, Tarquin has gone on the trail of Malcolm and Guin...

New-Age cult buys Greek Island

The tiny uninhabited Greek island of Pratinos has been bought by a recently formed cult, Renewal. The cult is led by a man known simply as *Guiding Light*, whose background and identity are obscure.

I'D BETTER FIND OUT HOW I GET TO THIS ISLAND...

WELCOME TO ATHENS INTERN...

DUTY FREE

INFORMATIO

PRATINOS?. WHERE THE RENEWAL PEOPLE ARE, YES?...

YOU'VE HEARD OF THEM?

INFORMA

SURE...THEIR PUBLICITY DEPARTMENT GAVE US THESE BROCHURES A FEW WEEKS AGO. ...HERE.... YOU CAN GET A BOAT FROM PIRAEUS.

INFORMA

Later....

CHUGGA CHUGGA CHUGGA CHUGGA

NOW LET'S HAVE A LOOK AT THIS BROCHURE... SEE WHAT THIS *RENEWAL* CULT IS ALL ABOUT...

RENEWAL

An Introduction to your PARADISE on EARTH

Tired of life's drudgery? Searching for Spirituality? COME TO PRATINOS AND JOIN **Renewal**

A message from our leader, GUIDING LIGHT, himself a star-child of our benevolent Alien Deity: "Greetings, Children of Renewal. May the peace among

The soon-to-be-completed TEMPLE COMPLEX, designed by GUIDING LIGHT, where you will live amongst a simple and loving community. Dressed in a natural hand-woven robe, you experience the feeling of deep

Artist's Impression

CRUMBS! I'VE GOT TO GET GUIN AWAY FROM THESE NUTTERS... IT'S INCREDIBLE THAT ANYONE FALLS FOR THIS RUBBISH...

EXCUSE ME!

EXCUSE ME, ARE YOU GOING TO THE RENEWAL SETTLEMENT TOO?

WELL..ER...SORT OF... I'M LOOKING FOR MY BRO...

AH YES! LOOKING FOR YOUR *SPIRITUAL DESTINY*, JUST LIKE US! LET US SHARE WITH YOU THE STORY OF OUR INNER JOURNEY...

An hour later....

...AND I WOKE UP ONE DAY AND REALISED THAT I COULDN'T FACE SPENDING THE REST OF MY LIFE LIVING IN READING, PROGRAMMING SOFTWARE FOR THE SEWAGE INDUSTRY...

THEN WE SENT OFF FOR THE RENEWAL VIDEO... GUIDING LIGHT SPOKE DIRECTLY TO US... IT WAS AN AMAZING EXPERIENCE

AMAZING...

JUST THINK! OUR CHANCE TO SHARE THE BUILDING OF GUIDING LIGHT'S PARADISE ON EARTH... FOR ONLY £40,000 EACH

HOW MUCH?!

I KNOW, IT'S AN UNBELIEVABLY LITTLE AMOUNT, ISN'T IT?.. BUT GUIDING LIGHT IS GRACIOUS ENOUGH TO RECIEVE MORE IF YOU WISH TO OFFER IT... WE'RE BOTH GIVING 60,000... LIKE IT SAYS IN THE VIDEO, YOU'RE REALLY GIVING TO YOUR OWN FUTURE...

NO WONDER HE COULD AFFORD TO BUY AN ISLAND...

HERE AT LAST!

I DON'T SEE ANYONE...

THEY'RE PROBABLY ALL UP AT THE TEMPLE, MEDITATING.

CAN'T YOU JUST FEEL THE TRANQUILLITY OF THE PLACE?

FUCKING BASTARDS!!

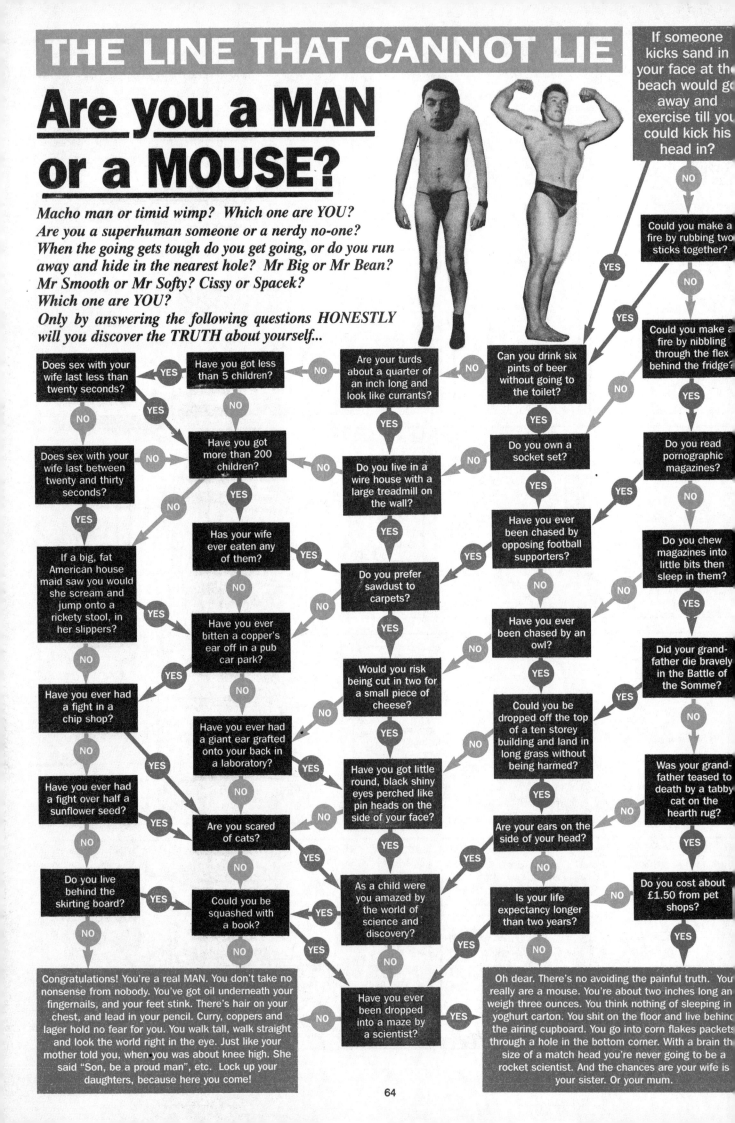

THE LINE THAT CANNOT LIE

Are you a MAN or a MOUSE?

Macho man or timid wimp? Which one are YOU?
Are you a superhuman someone or a nerdy no-one?
When the going gets tough do you get going, or do you run
away and hide in the nearest hole? Mr Big or Mr Bean?
Mr Smooth or Mr Softy? Cissy or Spacek?
Which one are YOU?
Only by answering the following questions HONESTLY
will you discover the TRUTH about yourself...

If someone kicks sand in your face at the beach would go away and exercise till you could kick his head in? — NO

Could you make a fire by rubbing two sticks together? — NO

Could you make a fire by nibbling through the flex behind the fridge? — YES

Do you read pornographic magazines? — NO

Do you chew magazines into little bits then sleep in them? — YES

Did your grandfather die bravely in the Battle of the Somme? — NO

Was your grandfather teased to death by a tabby cat on the hearth rug? — YES

Do you cost about £1.50 from pet shops? — YES

Does sex with your wife last less than twenty seconds? — YES

Have you got less than 5 children? — NO

Are your turds about a quarter of an inch long and look like currants? — NO

Can you drink six pints of beer without going to the toilet? — YES

Does sex with your wife last between twenty and thirty seconds? — NO

Have you got more than 200 children? — YES

Do you live in a wire house with a large treadmill on the wall? — NO

Do you own a socket set? — YES

Has your wife ever eaten any of them? — NO

Do you prefer sawdust to carpets? — YES

Have you ever been chased by opposing football supporters? — YES / NO

If a big, fat American house maid saw you would she scream and jump onto a rickety stool, in her slippers? — YES

Have you ever bitten a copper's ear off in a pub car park? — NO

Would you risk being cut in two for a small piece of cheese? — NO

Have you ever been chased by an owl? — YES / NO

Have you ever had a fight in a chip shop? — NO

Have you ever had a giant ear grafted onto your back in a laboratory? — YES

Have you got little round, black shiny eyes perched like pin heads on the side of your face? — YES

Could you be dropped off the top of a ten storey building and land in long grass without being harmed? — YES / NO

Have you ever had a fight over half a sunflower seed? — YES

Are you scared of cats? — NO

As a child were you amazed by the world of science and discovery? — YES

Are your ears on the side of your head? — NO

Do you live behind the skirting board? — YES

Could you be squashed with a book? — YES

Is your life expectancy longer than two years? — NO

Have you ever been dropped into a maze by a scientist? — YES / NO

Congratulations! You're a real MAN. You don't take no nonsense from nobody. You've got oil underneath your fingernails, and your feet stink. There's hair on your chest, and lead in your pencil. Curry, coppers and lager hold no fear for you. You walk tall, walk straight and look the world right in the eye. Just like your mother told you, when you was about knee high. She said "Son, be a proud man", etc. Lock up your daughters, because here you come!

Oh dear. There's no avoiding the painful truth. You really are a mouse. You're about two inches long and weigh three ounces. You think nothing of sleeping in a yoghurt carton. You shit on the floor and live behind the airing cupboard. You go into corn flakes packets through a hole in the bottom corner. With a brain the size of a match head you're never going to be a rocket scientist. And the chances are your wife is your sister. Or your mum.

64

Continued from page 57

DIANA: PRINCESS OF HEARTS

The sexational Royal Romance of the Century

Charles and Diana quickly became the most popular Royal couple since Victoria and Albert, and they were in constant demand to open things. Wherever they went crowds of adoring fans turned out to see them in their tens of thousands.

OFFICIAL OPENING
Summer 92

Isn't she lovely!

Aah, they look so happy together

Yes, she looks even more beautiful in real life

Mmm. And her nose looks a bit different too

But Diana was leading a tragic double life. She loved nothing more than to be at home with her two young Princes, William and Harry...

Corrr! One loves this!!!

Steady on Wills. One doesn't wish to fall orf

Come on Mum, let's see how high ones can bounce

But she hated work. Years of opening things and being given flowers were beginning to take their toll. Analysts of Royal body language began to read disturbing signs into the couples' public behaviour. Physical contact seemed cold, and there was seldom any eye contact between them. And little things, like Diana's awkwardly angled right foot in this picture suggested to many that their love affair was over.

But the watching public had no idea how bad things really were...

Whahey! Can I drive Dad? Which one's the horn?

And just where the hell do you think you're going with those kids?

GIORGIO

I'm going to bloody Scotland, aren't I. To do some paintings. Jesus! I'll need permission to wipe my friggin' arse next.

I hate it when Mummy and Deddy argue

Nag nag nag! Women eh? I never get a minutes peace!

Why are we always going to Scotland Daddy. It's boring!

No its not Harold. It's nice. We can go for walks and talk to the trees like we did last time

Trees are boring. I'd rather stay with Mummy. She does fun things like visiting tramps and going to pop concerts

65

Continues on page 72

GILBERT RATCHET

OH I DO LIKE TO BE BESIDE THE SEASIDE, READERS, OH I DO LIKE TO BE BESIDE THE SEA

OH I **DO** LIKE TO BE BESIDE AND SO FORTH

NOW THEN CHILDREN. TO GIVE YOUR PARENTS A BREAK FROM BEING CONTINUALLY SHOWN DULL AND UNINTERESTING SHELLS WHICH YOU FIND ON THE BEACH, WE'VE ORGANISED **A TREASURE HUNT**

I'M MAYOR ME

A HANDFUL OF CHEAP AND PATRONISING NICK-NACKS HAVE BEEN HIDDEN SOMEWHERE IN THE SAND

THIS IS A BRILLIANT IDEA FOR FINDING THAT TREASURE

I'VE BORROWED THIS GIANT ELECTRIC FAN FROM THE THEATRE, WHICH WILL BLOW AWAY THE TOP LAYER OF SAND, REVEALING THE GOODIES UNDERNEATH

AH-HAR ME HEARTIES, THAT TREASURE IS AS GOOD AS MINE

WHOOSH!

RAW SEWAGE Swimming Permitted anyway

OOPS! I DIDN'T NOTICE THAT NEARBY SEWAGE OUTLET

OH DEAR. THE MAYOR SEEMS TO HAVE COPPED MY "FAECES OF EIGHT"

SPLAT!

RAW SEWAGE

I AM BEDECKED WITH HUMAN EXCREMENT AND MY MAYORAL DIGNITY HAS BEEN COMPROMISED

PLEASE LEAVE THE BEACH

ON THE PROM

CUT'N'DRIED HAIRDRESSER

OODS 'N' RODS FISHING TACKLE

WANK YOU KINDLY ADULT BOOKS

HELLO, THIS GENT SEEMS TO BE IN A QUANDRY

I'M A STOCKBROKER, AND I'VE JUST LOST TWENTY PEE ON THE TUPPENNY WATERFALLS AMUSEMENT AR

THE STRESS IS SO GREAT THAT I'M GOING TO KILL MYSELF — BUT I CAN'T DECIDE WHICH METHOD OF SUICIDE TO USE

A HEFTY BLOW TO THE HEAD WITH THIS FRYING PAN SHOULD PROVIDE YOU WITH THE PERMANENT "EXECUTIVE RELIEF" YOU REQUIRE

FIRE AWAY, SON

SPANG!

WOPS! MY AIM WAS A LITTLE OFF. I'M AFRAID I MERELY CLIPPED YOUR NOSE, INSTEAD

NEVER MIND SON. AT LEAST YOU'VE RESTORED A PURPOSE TO MY LIFE...

...AND THAT IS TO BOOT YOU UP THE ARSE!

BOOT!

ON THE PIER

BUSINESS IS SLACK, GILBERT

MADAME EDITH FORTUNES TOLD £2

NOBODY WANTS THEIR FORTUNE TOLD TODAY

YOUR PROBLEM IS THAT PEOPLE AREN'T FEELING SUPERSTITIOUS ENOUGH

BUT MAYBE IF THEY SAW A GHOST, THAT WOULD PUT THEM IN THE RIGHT FRAME OF MIND TO COME AND SEE YOU. HMM.

DOWN THE STREET

CAREFUL WITH THIS GIANT STICK OF DYNAMITE WHICH WE'RE TAKING TO THE QUARRY, BERT

AYE. WE DON'T WANT TO DROP IT

YIKES! A GHOST...

...EERILY RESEMBLING A SMALL BOY WEARING A SHEET ON HIS HEAD

WOO! WOO!

AND SO

PALLADIUM THEATRE?

BOOM!

CRIMMINY! I'VE CAUSED THE LOCAL THEATRE TO BE REDUCED TO RUBBLE

PALLAD

I'M IN BIG TROUBLE THIS TIME

BUT THEN

WELL DONE YOUNG MAN! JIM DAVIDSON WAS DUE TO BE GIVING A PERFORMANCE IN THAT THEATRE TONIGHT

I'M £50

PLEASE ACCEPT THIS £50, WITH THE GRATITUDE OF ALL THE PEOPLE IN THIS TOWN

INSTEAD OF BUYING £50 WORTH OF FISH AND CHIPS I GAVE THE MONEY TO CHARITY, READERS, BECAUSE IT'S WRONG TO BE GREEDY

AND REMEMBER TO DRIVE CAREFULLY, GO TO CHURCH ON A REGULAR BASIS, AND ALWAYS RESPECT YOUR ELDERS

Ah, this is the life! A fortnight in Filey. Just the thing to take the weight off me Emma Freuds. They've been throbbing like Billy-Ho.

Yes dear.

Look out Nobby! Your deckchair 'A'-frame support ratchets haven't fully engaged on the...

Wha...?

SNAP!

AAAARGH! Bloody 'ell! Me Piles! They're being scissored in the mechanism!

Don't worry madam. I'll rescue your husband.

LIFEGUARD

Erm... could you try another way. That just looks like it's wedging them in tighter.

GRUNT. HEAVE.

MMF! MMF!

Right. This beach cricket bat should dislodge 'em.

THWACK! THWACK! THWACK!

GAAA! ME CHALFONTS!

K-POP!

THERE!

OH! WELL DONE!

Oh my word. His bumgrapes are in a terrible state.

I know. We'll lie him in the shade and let some air get to them. He'll be right as rain in no time.

LIFEGUARD

SO...

Two ninety-nines and a funny feet please.

ICES Mr.Whippycash

Sorry mate. I've not got no ice creams or lollies left. I'm off home.

BAH! ITS OVER A HUNDRED FARRUNHIGHT!

Right. Now that Nobby's safely in the shade, I can start "War And Peace" and read the whole book from cover to cover, giving it my undivided attention.

SEVERAL HOURS LATER...

"...THE MOST POWERFUL WEAPON OF IGNORANCE — THE DIFFUSION OF PRINTED MATERIAL. — THE END."

OOH. THAT WAS A GOOD BOOK. I THINK I'LL READ IT AGAIN. AHEM— PAGE ONE. "ALL HAPPY FAMILIES RESEMBLE ONE ANOTHER..."

SEVERAL HOURS LATER STILL...

"...BLAH BLAH BLAH - THE DIFFUSION OF PRINTED MATERIAL. — THE END."

OOH. THAT WAS A GOOD BOOK, NOBBY. OH DEAR- WHERE'S THE ICE-CREAM VAN GONE?

SPIT POP! CRACKLE HISS

IT WENT AGES AGO. YOUR HUSBAND'S FARMERS HAVE BEEN EXPOSED TO THE FULL MERCILESS HEAT OF THE SUN FOR A WHOLE DAY. THEY'RE BURNT TO A CRISP!

LIFEGUARD

TELL YOU WHAT- I'LL QUENCH THEM IN THE SEA.

PSSSSHHH!

G-AAAAAAAGH!

WOW! A GREATER BARB-TOOTHED BARACUDA - THE MOST TENACIOUS SPECIES OF SWORDFISH.

LIFEGUARD

AAARGH! AAARGH! AAARGH! AAARGH!

HEAVE! HEAVE!

R-R-R-RIP!

F...FF...FFF...

SHORTLY...

DOOH! AARGH! YOW! DOOH! AARGH! YOW! DOOH! AARGH! YOW! THEY'RE HANGING LIKE RIBBONS!

HANG ON NOBBY LOVE - I'LL GET THE OINTMENT OUT THE CUPBOARD. MIND, IT'S DARK IN HERE.

NOW LET'S SEE. EENY MEENY MINY MO...

PILE OINTMENT

DEVIL'S BRAND HELLFIRE JALAPENO SAUCE

SPLOSH

THERE. I'VE EMPTIED THE WHOLE BOTTLE ON 'EM.

NEXT DAY...

RIGHT. I'M KEEPING ME CHUFF OUT OF TROUBLE TODAY.

YES. LET'S HIRE A PEDALLO.

AND, NOT PARTICULARLY SURPRISINGLY...

OOPS. I FORGOT TO PUT THE CHAINGUARD BACK ON ONE OF THE PEDALLOS. THAT'LL LEAVE THE COGS EXPOSED BENEATH THE SLATTED PASSENGER SEAT.

WHICH BOAT?

NUMBER SIX.

Pedallo Hire £1 PER DAY

OH AYE. DEFINITELY SIX.

NO. HANG ON. I TELL A LIE. IT WASN'T NUMBER SIX...

IT WAS NUMBER TWO.

DRAG! GRIND! MESH! MANGLE! RIP!

YAAAAAARGH!!

OH NO - NOBBY'S IN TROUBLE WITH HIS PILES. I'D BEST PEDAL EXTRA-FAST BACK TO THE HARBOUR.

WE MUST BE CAUGHT IN A RIP TIDE. IT'S GETTING HARDER AND HARDER TO PEDAL.

GUMF

TWENTY MINUTES LATER...

I'M AFRAID HIS SIGMUNDS HAVE COMPLETELY PROLAPSED, MRS. PILES. THEY'VE GONE ROUND THE AXLE THIRTY-TWO TIMES. THEY'RE JAMMED FAST ON THE GANGLE-PIN AND CLOTTED ONTO THE GLIB-SHAFT.

FILEY COTTAGE HOSPITAL

NER! NER!

NER! NER!

CASUALTY

GOOD GRIEF! THIS IS THE WORST CASE OF PILES WRAPPED ROUND A PEDALLO AXLE I'VE SEEN SINCE 1975 - WHEN I STARTED THIS SHIFT. WE'RE GOING TO HAVE TO DO AN EMERGENCY OPERATION!

NEXT MORNING...

GOOD MORNING MR. PILES. IT WAS A 10-HOUR OPERATION. AND WE HAVE SUCCESSFULLY REMOVED THE COGS.

GET IN!

UNFORTUNATELY - IN DOING SO, WE HAD TO AMPUTATE YOUR HAEMORRHOIDS.

FUNNY. IT'S ALMOST AS IF I CAN STILL FEEL 'EM.

HOWEVER - AS LUCK WOULD HAVE IT, A ROAD ACCIDENT FATALITY WAS BROUGHT IN LAST NIGHT - AND HE WAS CARRYING A DONOR CARD.

WE MANAGED TO TRANSPLANT HIS PILES ONTO YOUR ARSE - AND THEY'VE TAKEN BEAUTIFULLY!

THEY'LL THROB LIKE BUGGERY FOR ABOUT SIX WEEKS UNTIL THE STITCHES HEAL... AND AFTER THAT, THEY'LL THROB LIKE BUGGERY.

Oliver Whore was a posh antique dealer who moved in Royal circles. One day he was working in his antique shop when the phone rang...

And for insurance purposes I'd say it's worth... er... around £5000

Really? That much eh? What a pleasant surprise

Oh, excuse me. I'll just answer the phone...

Hello, Oliver Whore Antiques. Furniture bought and sold - best prices paid. Full and part house clearances undertaken.

Pardon? Who is this? Goodness gracious! Is there any need for that?!

Look, this is the fifty third time you've called today! If you don't storp it I shall have no choice but to call the police, do you hear me?

Do you want to sniff my panties? Can you smell them? Can you smell my panties? You can't wait can you?

Coming up very soon some red hot panty sniffing sex action. But first of all here is a warning. The contents of this phone call are of a highly explicit and sexual nature.

The following day police called to see Diana.

I'm sorry Miss Diana. But when we dialled 1471 we got the number of a call box just round the corner from here.

How do you explain this Diana?

I can't explain it! I can't! But it wasn't me. It wasn't! You've got to believe me!

Late that evening Charles made a secret phone call...

Tampax calling Wicked Witch, over. Hi darling. That worked a treat! The police think it was her, and I swear she's cracking up. It won't be long now.

Charles and Camelia's plan was working to perfection. Within days the press turned on poor Diana, branding her a tramp and an unfit mother.

No! No! It's not true!! It's all lies!!

Then one day Diana came upon a milkman outside the Palace gates. Dressed in humble rags, the milkman did not recognise the beautiful Princess and spoke to her in common tongue.

I'll tell ya who's got Prince Charles' slippers under 'er bed. Only that Camelia Parker-Knowles! Yeah, he's been giving her one for *ages!* Fancy climbin' over Princess Di to get to 'er, eh? He must be maaaad!

At last it all began to make sense.

Brave Di wasn't going to give up her crown without a fight, and the next day she visited an old friend Andrew Motherwell

This story is Di-namite! It'll blow the lid off the Palace! I'll write a book this afternoon. Don't worry Diana, I'll make a fortune! I mean... I'll put your side of the story across.

One day Di was driving through Hyde Park when she spotted a tramp drowning in the Terpentine.

Help, help! I'm drowning!

Hold on, I'm coming!

Without a thought for her own safety Di bravely dived in and rescued the poor tramp

Thank you, Maam. You right saved me good and proper you did. Else wise I would have drowned and no mistake

Why, I'm naught but a humble tramp. And yet you risked your life to save me. You're an Angel of Mercy, Maam, to be sure. May the Lord bless you.

Fortunately for Diana a passing TV crew recorded the event.

The book's revelations and Di's acts of public kindness and bravery began to sway public opinion in her favour.

I think that Princess Di's great. She saved a tramp you know.

Yeah, and she visits tramps in cardboard boxes

That's right. Make a great Queen she would. Pity Charles is such a miserable old git. Talks to flowers and stuff, he does.

Meanwhile, as she sat down to a TV supper with her husband Brigadier Andrew Parker-Knoll, Camelia had a problem of her own...

Hoy! Camelia, isn't that your mate Prince Charles on the telly?

Erm... yes dear. Actually, before we watch this, there's something I think you ought to know

Charles had taken the unprecedented step of going on telly to answer questions from TV host Jonathon Dimbleby.

Now then, one thing I'm sure all the viewers would like to know Charles...

... Have you ever been unfaithful to Diana?

Erm... yes. I've been *doing it* with Camelia Parker-Knowles for ages. But only cos I wasn't getting any at home

CHARLES

That evening...

Good work Tampax! Better keep your head down cos the shit's really gonna hit the fan. My old man's already asked for a divorce. Now we just need to get rid of you-know-who... and I can be Queen at last!!

73

Continues on page 80

Million mile marathon nears end

AL JOLSON this week embarks on the final leg of a marathon million mile walk which has taken the tragic black singer a record 65 years to complete.

The walk came about after Jolson recorded the hit song 'Mammy', in which he vowed to walk a million miles for one his mammy's smiles. At first his devoted mother Eunice thought her all singing all dancing son was joking. But Jolson has spent an entire lifetime proving otherwise, turning his back on a glittering showbusiness career in order to prove his point.

Al Jolson arrives in Leicester on Wednesday

"Wait a minute. Wait a minute. You ain't seen nuthin' yet", says a tired black Al Johnson yesterday.

Walking

Jolson set off from Hollywood in 1931 and has been walking almost non-stop ever since. When his historic trek began Edgar Hoover was still president, pizzas had not been invented, and a Ford 'Model T' car cost just twelve dollars and fifteen cents. His epic journey has taken him through 165 countries, across the Himalayan mountains (eighteen times), through the hottest deserts, and even across thousands of miles of sea bed.

Crying

Along the way Jolson has got through 288,576 pairs of shiny black tap dancing shoes, lost 2,867 straw hats and 9,446 walking canes, and has changed his white cotton gloves no less than 189,545 times. Jolson has walked constantly, without sleep or food, managing to maintaining an average of 2 miles per hour despite ageing considerably over the years.

Sleeping

His journey was briefly interupted in 1939 by the outbreak of war. Unable to cross European borders the singer spent six years walking round in circles in a field in Ireland. When he eventually left locals clubbed together and raised enough cash to have a small statue erected in what has become known as 'Jolson's Field' near Letterkenny, to commemorate the singer's visit.

Talking

Jolson will this week clock up his millionth mile on British soil, having arrived through the Channel Tunnel from France yesterday. Ironically, his journey will end in Leicester - 4,500 miles from his mother's home in Carolina - but the singer will never-the-less be guaranteed a warm reception.

Living Doll

"This is a great honour for our city", said Deputy Lord Mayor Eric Thonks who will officially welcome the singer when he arrives at the DeMontford Hall on Wednesday afternoon. "My wife and I are big fans of his, and we will be inviting Mr Jolson to unveil a plaque to commemorate his great feat of endurance."

Mile End tube etc.

There is however a tragic side to the story. When Mr Jolson arrives he will be told that his mammy died in 1932, only 9 weeks after he set off on his mammoth hike.

Man dies in think tank

AN inquest has heard how a man who died in a Government think tank had not been wearing protective breathing apparatus.

Frank Ramsbottom, 52, was found dead inside the think tank, at Reading, Oxfordshire, in May of last year. He had been cleaning the tank when the accident occurred.

Ladder

Fellow worker Jack Higgins told the inquiry how he had attempted to pull Mr Ramsbottom out of the tank after his colleague collapsed, but was unable to carry him up a narrow ladder. He was eventually driven back by noxious ideas and ran to get help. Neither men had been wearing breathing apparatus at the time.

Inquest hears how safety rules were not followed

A Government spokesman said it was standard procedure for maintenance men to wear breathing apparatus when entering a think tank. But he could not confirm that the men had been issued with suitable equipment on that occasion. Stringent safety rules were applied and suitable training given, but he added that it was not always possible to ensure that correct procedures were being followed.

Hose

The think tank was being cleaned out in readiness for a delivery of new ideas and concepts. It was a routine operation carried out every 2 months, and there had been no reported incidents of this type in the past.

Leder

A home office pathologist confirmed that Mr Ramsbottom had died after inhaling a large quantity of toxic thoughts. He said a thin residue of ideas was found on the bottom of the tank and that Mr Ramsbottom would have died within minutes. The coroner recorded a verdict of accidental death and recommended that procedures for cleaning out think tanks be reviewed in the light of the accident.

Hosen

A man was killed whilst trying to unblock a brain drain at Dublin University last week. Thomas McDonnagh, 27, had lowered himself through a manhole and was attempting to remove leaves and other debris when he was swept away by a torrent of brains. His body was later recovered from the river Liffey.

Foreskin gives up treasures

In an adventure story straight out of Indiana Jones a team of American scientists have recovered lost treasures hidden behind the foreskin of American actor Anthony Quinn.

Helmet

Tales of lost treasures buried deep beneath the actor's helmet have been rife in Hollywood for over half a century. And last year a team of scientists from the University of California set out on a pioneering expedition to explore the unchartered area known as 'Quinn's Polo Neck', and salvage items rumoured to have been lost there over the years.

Old King

Several items were successfully recovered by the expedition but the finds were not as spectacular as had been hoped. The items recovered, which have been put on display at the Institute of Foreskin Research in Glendale, California, included a large piece of cheese, thought to be 42 years old, and some fluff.

Andy Andy

Evidence suggested that the Greek actor, born ironically in Rejkvik, Iceland, to Mexican parents, may have been ransacked by bell end robbers in the early nineteen fifties.

Billy Quizz

ONE NIGHT...

BUMP! THUMP!

BILLY... BILLY... DID YOU HEAR THAT? THERE'S SOMEONE DOWNSTAIRS. GO AND HAVE A LOOK

EH!? WASSAT?

THERE'S SOMEONE IN THE HOUSE, BILLY... A BURGLAR!

OH, RIGHT... I'LL GO AND SEE

I WONDER WHO IT IS... HMM...

...THE FLOCK WALLPAPER...

...THE SPORTY PICTURES...

WHO WOULD BREAK INTO A HOUSE LIKE THIS?

MR. BURGLAR...

...COME ON DOWN

HA! HA! HA! HAAAAAA!

NOW THEN, YOU'RE JIM... JIM THE BURGLAR... YOU'VE BEEN BURGLING FOR TWENTY FIVE YEARS... YOU'RE MARRIED TO PAT AND YOU HAVE TWO LOVELY SONS, LEFTY AND NOSHER... ALSO BURGLARS

HUNH!?

I'LL BET IT'S PORRIDGE FOR BREAKFAST IN YOUR HOUSE, EH?

...SUIT YERSELVES... NOW, JIM, IT SAYS HERE THAT YOU MET PAT WHILE BURGLING HER PARENTS HOUSE IN 1963 AND YOU MARRIED TWO YEARS LATER... THAT'S LOVELY...

...YOU BROKE INTO HER HOUSE AND STOLE HER HEART... ANYWAY, IT'S LOVELY TO HAVE YOU HERE AND YOU'VE DONE VERY WELL SO FAR, JIM... SO LET'S GO OVER TO THE TABLE AND SEE WHAT YOU'VE GOT...

THERE'S A STATE OF THE ART VIDEO RECORDER... GRANDAD'S SOLID GOLD CARRIAGE CLOCK... A BEAUTIFUL SILVER CANTEEN OF CUTLERY...

SWAG

Little bit closer, Jim... bit closer... just there... smashing...

A 35mm FULLY AUTOMATIC CAMERA... A CANDLEABRA... A CUT CRYSTAL DECANTER...

...AND OF COURSE, THERE'S YOUR £750 IN CASH...

...NOW THEN, JIM...

...WOULD YOU LIKE TO GAMBLE WHAT YOU'VE STOLEN TONIGHT, ON THE CONTENTS OF THAT TEAPOT? I DON'T KNOW WHAT'S IN IT, JIM... COULD BE THE KEYS TO A FABULOUS HATCHBACK IN THE GARAGE... COULD BE TICKETS FOR A DREAM CARIBBEAN HOLIDAY FOR YOU AND YOUR WIFE PAT...

...BUT STEADY ON, JIM...

...IT COULD BE TONIGHT'S BOOBY PRIZE...

...AN OLD TEABAG!

SO WHAT'S IT TO BE, JIM?

...ARE YOU GOING TO GAMBLE? YOU'VE GOT THE TIME IT TAKES FOR ME TO FETCH THE TEAPOT TO DECIDE, JIM, AND THAT TIME STARTS...

...NOW!

BOOP BI-DOOP BI-DOOP! BOOP BI-DOOP BI-DOOP! BOOP BI-DOOP BI-DOOP! BOOP BI-DOOP BI-DOOP!

BOOP BI-DOOP BI-DOOP! BOOP BI-DOOP BI-DOOP! BOOP BI-DOOP BI-DOOP! BOOP BI-DOOP BI-DOOP!

BOOP BI-DOOP BI-DOOP! BOOP BI-DOOP BI-DOOP! BI-DIP!..D-DIP!.. DIDDLY DOOP!..

...PYOOOOOOW!

WELL, JIM... WHAT'S YOUR DECISION?

I...ER...

...HE'S GOING TO GAMBLE...

...COME ON EVERYBODY, GIVE A BIG HAND TO JIM THE BURGLAR!

LET'S SEE WHAT HE'S WON...

OH, JIM... OH DEAR, JIM... JIM...

OH, JIM, JIM, JIM, JIM, JIM!

YOU'VE WON...

...TONIGHT'S JACKPOT SWAG... MY WIFE'S JEWELS!

YES! THESE FABULOUS HEIR LOOM JEWELS HAVE BEEN IN THE FAMILY FOR 60 YEARS...

...AND YOU'RE GOING TO WALK AWAY WITH THEM TONIGHT! CONGRATULATIONS, JIM, YOU'VE BEEN A TERRIFIC BURGLAR. GIVE MY LOVE TO PAT AND HAVE A SAFE JOURNEY HOME...

SWAG

DIDN'T HE DO WELL?

NEXT DAY...

OKAY, MR. QUIZZ. WE'VE GOT SOME SUSPECTS ON AN IDENTITY PARADE. WOULD YOU LIKE TO SEE IF YOU CAN PICK YOUR BURGLAR OUT?

YES... OF COURSE...

...HI!... I USED TO WORK IN A FLOWER SHOP. IF YOU WERE TO BUY ME FLOWERS, WHAT TYPE WOULD YOU BUY AND WHY?...

1 2 3

...AND THAT'S FOR BURGLAR NUMBER... TWO, PLEASE!

75

Raffles *The Gentleman Thug*

I SAY, RAFFLES OLD CHAP, SHAKE A LEG. THE CAB'S WAITING TO TAKE US TO LORD MARCHMONT'S BALL. YOU DON'T WANT TO KEEP THE HONORABLE MISS FFORBES-HAMPTON-FFORBES' WAITING.

VERY WELL BUNNY.

NOW - LET'S SEE. HAVE I REMEMBERED EVERYTHING? PRISTINE WHITE GLOVES, SHINY TOPPER, SILK-LINED OPERA CLOAK, SILVER-TOPPED CANE, STANLEY KNIFE...?

STANLEY KNIFE!? GOOD HEAVENS RAFFLES! WHAT THE DEVIL FOR?

IN CASE THERE'S ANY TROUBLE. REMEMBER LAST MONTH'S RECEPTION AT THE REFORM CLUB - WHEN I GOT INTO THAT FIGHT WITH THE BISHOP OF WORCESTER. IF I HADN'T LACED HIM UP HE MIGHT HAVE BITTEN OFF ME EAR, BEGAD!

WELL - YOU STARTED IT RAFFLES.

MY DEAR CHAP - HE WAS LOOKING AT ME FUNNY, AND AS EDWARDIAN LONDON SOCIETY'S PREMIER GENTLEMAN THUG IT WAS MY DUTY TO START ON HIM. YOU KNOW THAT AS WELL AS I DO.

HERE WE ARE GENTLEMEN - MARCHMONT MANSIONS. THAT'LL BE TWO AND SIX IN THE OLD MONEY, GUV.

HERE'S THREE SHILLINGS MY GOOD MAN.

THAT'S WERY KIND OF YOU SQUIRE.

'SCUSE ME GUV'NOR. IS THIS YOUR SCARF, SIR?

THIS, SIR, IS A LINEN SCARF. DO I LOOK LIKE THE SORT OF MAN WHO WOULD WEAR A LINEN SCARF?

I JUST FOUND IT ON THE FLOOR, GUV...

...I THOUGHT IT MIGHT...

MY SCARVES ARE FASHIONED OF THE FINEST SILK, SIR. ANY MAN WHO SUGGESTS DIFFERENTLY IS A CUNT.

COME ON THEN. COME ON. ARE YOU A FUCKIN' PUFF THEN? COME ON. STICK ONE ON THERE. COME ON THEN. WHAT YOU WAITING FOR?

SORRY GUV. I DON'T WANT NO TROUBLE.

OOF!

CLACK!

PUNCH! PUNCH! PUNCH!

HAVE YOU HAD ENOUGH, EH? HAVE YOU FUCKIN' HAD ENOUGH, SIR?

I SAY RAFFLES OLD CHAP, YOU CERTAINLY SHOWED THAT IMPUDENT FELLOW A CLEAN SET OF FISTICUFFS, WHAT!

INDEED BUNNY. HE'LL NOT HASTEN TO TANGLE WITH RAFFLES AGAIN AND THAT'S FOR SURE.

INSIDE... AH - MISS FFORBES-HAMPTON-FFORBES. I HOPE YOU WILL FORGIVE MY GROSS IMPERTINENCE WHEN I INFORM YOU OF HOW DELIGHTFUL YOUR APPEARANCE IS THIS EVENING.

WHY THANK-YOU LORD RAFFLES. YOUR COMPLIMENTS ARE RECIPROCATED.

SHALL WE GO IN?

LORDS, LADIES AND GENTLEMEN. LORD RAFFLES AND MISS FFORBES-HAMPTON-FFORBES.

AH - MISS FFORBES-HAMPTON-FFORBES, HAVE YOU HAD THE PLEASURE OF BEING INTRODUCED TO HIS IMPERIAL EXCELLENCY THE MOLDAVIAN AMBASSADOR?

PLOVSKY PLIVSKY PLOVSK DUBROVSKY PLOV.

HIS EXCELLENCY SAYS HE IS DELIGHTED TO MEET YOU AGAIN LORD RAFFLES.

COULD YOU TELL HIS EXCELLENCY THAT LIKEWISE I AM DELIGHTED TO MEET HIM.

PLIVSKY PLOV BOV PLOVSKY PLOVSKY BOVSK PLOVOLOVSKY.

PLOVSKY PLOV PLOV BLOVSKY PLOV BOV.

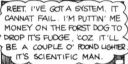

TITS OOT FOR THE LADS

HOW SID, ARE YE COMIN' OOT? WUZ ARE AALL OFF OOT FOR TO CELEBRATE COZ JOE RECKONS HE'S REMEMBERED HIS JOKE.

ERM, WELL, ACTUALLY I'M WAALKIN' OOT WI' A REALLY FANCY LADY.

OH AYE?

AYE. SHE DOESN'T HALF GAN. LAST TIME I TOOK 'ER OOT SHE WAS SNIFFIN' ROOND ME BOLLOCKS, MAN. I TELL YE WHAT ELSE, SHE'S WORTH A FORTUNE.

AYE.

TWO DWAAFS, ONE POOF. TWO DWAAFS, ONE POOF. TWO DWAAFS, ONE POOF.

AYE. AN' I HEAR SHE LOVES IT DOGGY STYLE!

LATER...
AND IN TRAP No. 6 "FANCY LADY", OWNED AND TRAINED BY SHORTY McDEE.

MEANWHILE...
WHAT A SMASHIN' IDEA, EH? COMIN' TO THE DOGS. PITY SID NEVER COME OOT. HE'LL HAVE HIS HANDS FULL MIND!

TURNSTILES

TWO DWAAFS, ONE POOF... ERM... AN' A VICAR...

REET. I'VE GOT A SYSTEM. IT CANNAT FAIL. I'M PUTTIN' ME MONEY ON THE FORST DOG TO DROP IT'S FUDGE, 'COZ IT'LL BE A COUPLE O' POOND LIGHTER. IT'S SCIENTIFIC MAN.

WELL, WHY DIVVEN'T YE PUT IT ON THAT ONE, IT'S HAVIN' A SHITE NOO.

AYE THAT ONE WHAT'S WITH THE BLURK WHAT LOOKS LIKE SID.

! ! !

!

WHAAAH! HAH! HAH! HA! HEH! HEH! HEH!

WHAY-HEY! FANCY FUCKIN' LADY INDEED!

HE AALWEZ GETS DOGS, BUT THEY'VE USUALLY GOT TWO LEGS!

SID'S NEW BORD'S A FUCKIN' HOOND!

AYE. I HORD SHE'S A REET FUCKIN' BITCH!

FUCK OFF! FUCK OFF! LEAVE US ALAIRN! I'M ONLY DEEIN' THIS FOR ME MATE!... I'M SEEIN' THE BORD LATER! ... HONEST MAN!

HOW SID! SHE'S AN IMPROVEMENT ON THAT ONE YE CHATTED UP LAST WEEK, EH? HA! HA! HA! HA!

AYE. BUT NOT AS HAIRY!

SQUICH!

AAIIYAH!

WRENCH!

SHORTLY...
GET YERSEL' IN THERE AN' GET FIXED UP SIDNEY. WE'LL PICK YE UP LATER, WE'RE GANNIN' TU THE BAR.

ACCIDENT AND EMERGENCY

TEE HEE!

SNIGGER!

SO, WHAT'S THE PROBLEM?

I THINK I'VE BUST ME ANKLE. I FELT NOWT MIND. I'M ROCK.

THROB!

AND HOW DID IT HAPPEN?

ERM... I SLIPPED... IN ... SORT OF TROD... ERM, THERE WAS THIS BIG...

... PARACHUTIN', AYE, SEE ME CHUTE NEVER URPENED.

OKAY. THIRD CUBICLE ON THE LEFT.

ONE, TWO, THREE, AYE, THIS UN.

DOCTOR? I'M NOT A ...

OOH DOCTOR AT LAST.

IT'S MY BREASTS. I'VE FALLEN AWKWARDLY AND HURT THEM. COULD YOU CHECK THEM FOR DAMAGE, PLEASE.

UMPH!

TREMBLE!   TREMBLE!

DO THEY FEEL ALL RIGHT THEN DOCTOR?

GUMPH! AYE... FUCKIN' SMASHIN'!

HELLO GRIPPER, LOVE. IT'S OKAY, THE DOCTOR HAS HAD A GOOD FEEL OF THEM AND HE SAYS THEY'RE ABSOLUTELY FINE.

mmmmh.

UH?

UGH!?

BROUGH PARK GREYHOUND STADIUM

10 MINUTES LATER...
AYE LOVE. PARACHUTIN' AGAIN. CHUTE STUCK. LANDED IN A SCRAPYARD, SEE.

Magna Carty

Soap star's fatal attraction

BBC CHIEFS have banned a leading EastEnders star from the set of the top TV soap after he became magnetic. According to insiders Todd Carty, who plays Mark Fowler in the long running drama, began to attract metal objects last month, wreaking havoc on the set of the four times weekly soap.

HICCUP

"Filming schedules are so tight even the smallest hiccup can cause major problems", our source told us. "When Carty began to attract small metal objects during filming it became a nightmare. Two minute scenes were taking two days to shoot".
One brief scene in the Queen Vic pub where Carty walked in and said "hello" to landlady Peggy Mitchell, alias bubbly former Carry On actress Babs Windsor, took eight hours to film after a metal ashtray began sliding along the bar towards him.
In another incident Carty caused damage to a video tape he was sitting next to and an entire scene had to be re-shot at considerable expense. Eventually bosses were forced to act when magnetic Carty turned up for work with paper clips stuck to his face. He has since been told to stay away from the EastEnders studios until his condition is cured.

COCK UP

If Carty remains magnetic his TV acting career would almost certainly be over. However there is a chance that he could still act at the North pole, because magnets don't work there.
Carty was last night stuck to his fridge door, and unable to answer the phone.

❑ NEWS in a little BOX

Computer users faced severe delays yesterday after after a lorry shed its load on the Information Superhighway, in the Silcon Valley just east of Swindon. The Internet was closed for six hours as a result of the accident.

HEAVEN'S ABOVE

Afterlife gossip with the late ☆☆ *Fanny Batter* ☆☆

*After dying of liposuction in a top Beverly Hills clinic our regular Hollywood gossip columnist Fanny Batter now reports **EXCLUSIVELY** from Heaven.*

★ Rumours of a romance between dead Doctor Who **Jon Pertwee** and **Marilyn Monroe** have spread after they were seen together at the exclusive **St. Pauls** restaurant in fashionable Heaven's Gate. Pals say the couple, who met at Jon's recent cloud warming party, are strictly 'just good friends'. *Don't you believe it!*

★ Get this! Word in Paradise is that rock god **Freddy Mercury** has gone *straight*. Sorry to disappoint you, fellas! So who's the lucky lady? None other than former TV dog trainer **Barbara Woodhouse**. Pals of the former wild man say Freddy is a reformed character. Could it be that Babs has finally got him house trained? *Watch this space!*

★ Hell raiser **River Phoenix** is in trouble again after angels were called out to the Cobra Club, his exclusive celebrity watering hole in Hell, after former EastEnders star **Pete Beal** was found slumped unconscious under a table. Last year **Sir Matt Busby** was found dead outside the club on two separate occasions after drinking potentially lethal cocktails of heroin and ambrosia.

★ Former King of Rock'n'Roll **Elvis Presley** has made a new fortune - *selling sewing machines!* Presley built his new business up from scratch after arriving in Heaven 20 years ago without a nickel to his name. Entrepreneur Elvis is now rumoured to be worth a cool $500 million and has been linked romantically with a host of Heavenly bodies, most recently tragic tuna sandwich stunner **Momma Cass**.

★ *"Hey you! Get off of my cloud!"* That's what Rolling Stone **Brian Jones** has told dead fans who've been squatting in the grounds of his exclusive $500,000 Heaven mansion. Elsewhere excited Stones fans queued overnight to buy tickets for a planned **Keith Richards** show in Paradise Park. But the star failed to show up, and thousands of dead butterflies due to be released at the gig died again.

★ *Can you keep a secret?* Word from **Fanny Craddock**'s exclusive $800 a head 'Cloud Nine' restaurant is that **H.R.H. The Queen Mother** is already booked in for her 100th birthday bash in the year 2000! But get this! Fireworks will fly when her own mum, **Queen Victoria**, discovers she's not on the guest list! According to dead royal insiders the Queen Mum disapproves of Victoria's current toy boy lover **John Wayne**.

Missing you already! *Fanny* x

Get back on your feet from just £39*

It's everyone's nightmare. You're walking alone at night in an unfamiliar area and your shoes suddenly break down. What do you do? Attempt to repair them yourself? Abandon your footwear on the pavement and struggle home in your socks? Well, now there's a third option. National Shoe Breakdown rescue service.

Membership of **NATIONAL SHOE BREAKDOWN** entitles you to:

● **Pathside assistance.** Trained cobblers on call 24 hours a day, 7 days a week. Over 85% of breakdowns fixed on the spot whether its a loose heel, snapped lace, flapping sole or something in your shoe.

● **Complete cover,** even when you're wearing someone else's footwear. **You're** the member, **not** the shoes.

● **Priority** to members in vulnerable situations, such as lone women who have trod in a dog turd.

● **Relay service.** If the fault cannot be rectified on the pavement we'll get you and your shoes to your destination.

● **Replacement footwear.** If your shoes cannot be repaired within 24 hours, we'll provide courtesy flip flops for up to 7 days.

● **HOMESTART.** Can't find one of your slippers in the morning? Our qualified shoesmiths will be round to look under the sofa, or retrieve it from the dog's mouth.

To join, call us **now** on
0000 994 388
Calls cost 95p per minute cheap rate

*£39 is the cost of standard cover which does not include RELAY or HOMESTART and may not apply to certain high performance shoes such as hand-stiched Italian pigskin brogues or crocodile loafers.

Continued from page 73

At Windsor Castle the Queen was far from happy.

I fancy shooting something this weekend

Well you bleedin' can't. Charles and Di have had another bust-up and we've got the kids for the weekend. Come on Edward, give me a hand with these dishes.

Shortly, as they left the castle...

It's a bloody nuisance this. Third weekend in a row

I know. I don't mind babysitting once in a while, but this is getting ridiculous

Did I turn the chip pan off?

I'm sure you did love

Mmmm. That's funny that. I could have sworn I smelled something burning

When the Windsors arrived back the following day fireman were still putting their castle out.

Don't worry love. The insurance will cover it

It's not insured

Well, it's not our castle then, is it? Belongs to the tax payers. *They* can pay for the bastard.

Bloody hell Phil. What horrible anus! What ca go wrong next, eh?

But even as the Queen spoke, an altogether different anus was about to hit the headlines. For unbeknown to Princess Di, her innocent visit to a Soho massage parlour was being filmed by an evil Australian porn magnate using secret cameras hidden in an air vent.

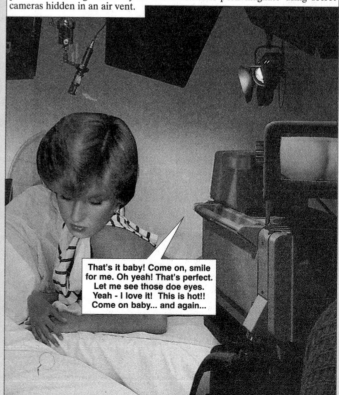

That's it baby! Come on, smile for me. Oh yeah! That's perfect. Let me see those doe eyes. Yeah - I love it! This is hot!! Come on baby... and again...

80

The story continues on page 88

BOO-YAKA! BOO-YAKA! GET SORTED FOR **TEES** WITH A RAVEY DAVEY TEE-SHIRT. SEE PAGE 39 FOR DETAILS

Charlie PONTOON

The MAN that MATTERS

How dare Germans call our cows mad? Cows may not be as clever as monkeys, but you don't need 'A' levels to be made into sausages. No doubt the Germans would have us eating foreign food if they had their way.

Well I've eaten foreign food, and paid the price. It's not a pleasant business.

The Germans should keep their mouths shut and stick to what they're good at - making cuckoo clocks.

★★★★★★★★★★★★★★★★★★★

So. Fat, bad mannered, American golfer John Daly has bought his own private jet. He tells us it is safer travelling by private plane than it is on public flights.

Try telling that to Buddy Holly.

★★★★★★★★★★★★★★★★★★★

I'm sick and tired of farmers who tell us they are over worked and under paid. What nonsense. If they cut their grass every weekend, like the rest of us, they wouldn't face such an enormous task when they eventually get round to doing it - about once a year, judging by the state of some of their farms.

An hour or so invested on a Sunday afternoon would save them weeks of messing around with tractors and combine harvesters.

Is it any wonder cows go mad, having to live with these fat, lazy, ignorant people?

★★★★★★★★★★★★★★★★★★★

The so called 'experts' tell us that 'air quality' is getting worse because of the ozones. What will they think of next? *Well I went for a walk in my garden this morning and the air was perfectly alright.*

These ozone moaners are the same people who would have us living in tree houses instead of driving cars to work if they had their own way.

If these long haired layabouts can't breath properly, perhaps they should stop sticking drugs up their noses, and try doing a decent day's work for a change.

* The Man In The Pub has gone to the toilet and will be back in October.

What a load of warlocks!

A leaked copy of the new Labour manifesto has provoked uproar in the Commons. The two page document was faxed anonymously to the office of Tory back bencher Sir Anthony Regents-Park who immediately branded it 'mumbo jumbo'. And he has attacked Labour's plans to use witchcraft and black magic as their main weapons in the battle against high inflation and unemployment.

NONSENSE

"It is a nonsense that a Labour government could seek to reduce public spending by using a hotch potch of spells and enchantments such as those outlined in this document", Sir Anthony told reporters yesterday.

POPPYCOCK

The document outlines Tony Blair's plans to use traditional mediaeval sorcery combined with Afro-Caribean voodoo rituals to turn around the British economy in a matter of seconds, creating millions

of jobs, new houses, and better schools. Plans to wipe out NHS waiting lists using an incantation were branded "totally impractical" by Sir Anthony.

TULIPFANNY

Throughout the document, entitled 'Labra Cadabra! It's New Labour', party leader Tony

Blair is referred to as the 'Chief High Wizard of the Dark Power' and members of his cabinet as 'Sorcerers'. Among its main goals are the successful introduction of European monetary union and a peaceful solution to the political crisis in Northern Ireland. Mr Blair is quoted as saying that a spell could be cast upon our European colleagues which would cause them to agree with all of our arguments. And he suggests that a special potion could be brewed and sprinkled on the waring factions in Northern Ireland, bringing fighting to an end.

BLUEBELLMINGE

It was rumoured that the late Harold Wilson dabbled in the occult in a fruitless attempt to solve the bread strike of 1973, a claim which his widow Mrs Wilson, strongly denies.

84

COCKNEY WANKER

ORWIGHT DARLIN'

GAWD LAV A DACK! I'VE NOT KNOCKED OUT NO JAM JARS FOR THE LARST TEN BLEEDIN' MINUTES...

...I'M FED AP!

WANKER'S MOTORS
QUALITY USED CARS

· OFFICE

CAR OF THE WEEK

CAR OF THE WEEK

I FANCY A NARCE LITTLE BOOZER DAHN THE EAST END. I CAN SEE OUR NAMES ABOVE THE RORY O'MORE...WANKAH AN' SHIRL...

...LICENCED TO SELL INTOXICATIN' LIQUORS. HA! LAVERLY JABBERLY!

SO... IS THAT WALFORD INSURANCE? I WANT TO AP THE COVER ON ME CAR LOT, MY SAN

WOT? 'OW MATCH IS IT?

ER...DUNNO 'OW MATCH DOES A NARCE LITTLE RAB-A-DAB COST?

A CAPPLE OF 'UNDRED BAGS OF SAND, SAMFINK LIKE THAT

RIGHT! AP IT T' THAT, THEN

LLOYDS OF LONDON

EROLL FLYNN

SCREAM & SHOUT

SORTED!

KNOCKAAHT! OH, AN' CAN YOU SEND ME A CLAIM FORM JAST IN CASE THE FACKIN' PLACE BURNS TO THE GRAAHND IN ABAAHT TEN MINUTES TIME?

YEH! NO TRABBLE

PETROL

CHEERS, CHIEF!...LISTEN, I'VE GOT TO GO, I FINK I CAN SMELL SMOKE

HALF AN HOUR LATER...

GAW! FACKIN' 'ELL WANKAH! THAT APPIN' YER COVER JAST BEFORE THE FIRE. 'ERE'S YER CHEQUE FOR A CAPPLE OF CENTURIES WORF OF BAGS OF SAAAND!

WAS A STWOKE A LACK, WONNIT, EH? 'ERE'S YER CHEQUE FOR A CAPPLE OF CENTURIES WORF OF BAGS OF SAAAND!

HEH! HEH! 'AAAANSOME!

THE HOSKINS ARMS

FIZZY BREWERS

SNAG

WOTCHA, JOHN...I'LL 'AVE A PINT-A FIZZY, A BAG OF PAWK SCRATCHIN'S AND THE PUB

RIGHT, THAT'S TEN QUID FOR THE BEER, TWO SIXTY FOR THE SCWATCHIN'S AN TWO 'ANDRED GWAND FOR THE WAB-A-DAB

THERE YOU GO, MY SAN.

RIGHT. I'M ORF! THE KEYS ARE IN THE DOOR...

...THE BINMEN CAM ON WEDNESDAYS, THE BREWERY DROP THE BEER OFF ON MANDAYS AN' THE KRAYS GIVE YOU A CHELSEA SMILE ON SATURDAYS

LAVERLY JABBERLY. I FINK THAT'S EVERYFINK I NEED TO KNOW

A WEEK LATER...

PINT-A APPLE FRITTER CHIEF...AN' A BAG-A NATS!

OVER 'ERE CHIEF...PINT-A APPLE FRITTER AN' A BAG-A NATS

Y'KNOW, SHIRL...I'M STILL NOT 'APPY, I'M NOT. I'M BEGINNIN' T' REALISE IT WASN'T THE CAR LOT THAT I WAS PISSED OFF WIV...

...IT WAS THE ROUTINE...IT WAS LANDON! SAME OLD PEOPLE... SAME OLD FACES. I WANT T' SEE SAMFINK OF THE WORLD BEFORE I GET TOO OLD... SPEND A BIT OF TIME IN THE SAN!..

THE HOSKINS ARMS

FIZZY BREWERIES

... I MEAN, LOOK AT THIS BLADDY WEVAH... NON STOP MICHAEL CAINE ALL DAY...

... LET'S PACK 'AP AN' GO TO SPAIN. SEE 'OW OTHER PEOPLE LIVE... ... BROADEN OUR 'ORIZONS. WE NEED A CHANGE FROM ALL THIS

WOT? YOU MEAN SELL THE PAB, WANKAH?

SLAP!

DON'T TAWLK SCHTYOOOPID. I'D NEVAH SELL THIS PLACE...

HALF AN HOUR LATER...

'ERE Y'GO, WANKAH... STICK THAT IN YER SKY WOCKET...

GOOD JOB YOU 'APPED YER COVER LARST NIGHT, INNIT

THE HOSKINS ARMS

WOTCHU GOIN'T'DO...OPEN IT AP AGAIN, EH, OR WOT?

NAH! WE'RE FED AP WIV LANDON. WE'RE GOIN'T' SPAIN...MEET NEW PEOPLE ...SEE 'OW THEY LIVE... SOAK AP THEIR CALTURE

SO... PINT-A APPLE FRITTER, CHIEF... AN A BAG-A NATS!

WANKERS ENGLISH PUB

NO DAGOS

GPD ST. 9. 96

VIZ 80

Continued from page 80

Diana
Princess of Hearts Part 3

In the wake of Andrew Motherwell's revealing book and Diana's exposure on TV, the reluctant Princess suddenly found herself in the media spotlight. Suffering from enormous personal stress she had turned to star gazing shrink Mystic Meg for help.

Where are we going mommy?

We're going to see my analyst.

Oh no, not her again. She's a loony.

What's this? Oh no! The press are waiting outside, and I'm wearing trousers. Damn it!

But everywhere she went pepperami photographers lay in wait. Life became a never ending game of cat and mouse. And Diana was the cheese.

More than anything she yearned for privacy.

At last I've managed to burn off the press and my police escort. Alone at last!

Unknown to her pursuers, Diana was hiding a tragic secret. Under the terrific glare of the public spotlight the fragile Princess had begun to wilt. She was suffering from a rare skin condition known as celluloid, caused by over exposure of the legs to camera flash lights.

CHELSEA HARBER
POSH GYM 4 TOFFS

The only cure was exercise, and so every day Diana headed to an exclusive Chelsea health club where she could work out in privacy, away from the prying eyes and lenses of the press.

I've had enough of this life on the run, constantly running and hiding from the press.

I've made my mind up. I'm going to cancel all my public duties, and I'm going to do it today!

Diana called her press secretary from the gym.

Cancel all my public engagements! Everything! I'm retiring from public life, starting from NOW!

Oh, and tell the picture editor at the News of the World I'll be using the dumbbells by the pool in about thirty minutes.

That's it love... let's see those eyes... perfect!

Turn this way a little Di... that's great!

Sky News Di. Can you give us a little sexy grunt as you lift your arm love?

The sparkle had gone from the Royal relationship. Diana longed to be loved, but in bed Charles was moody and unresponsive.

One doesn't fency heving sex tonight, does one Charles?

Can't one see, one is reading a book! Now be quiet and go to sleep.

But for the sake of the children they tried to maintain normal family life.

Phooar! Look at page three! Can I have Joanne Guest for my birthday?

No William. You had a model last year. How about a rugby player instead?

The young Prince was given England captain Will Carling for his birthday, and Carling set about teaching the future king to play rugby. But the Prince was a reluctant pupil.

Here... take the ball. Then run with it, okay?

No, I prefer this ball. It's round, see. So it rolls.

Ooyah!

Urggh! I've got him!

Man on! (Or whatever they say in rugby)

But Di enjoyed Carling's company, and she often joined in with his games. She was always a competitive girl, and now - starved of love - she enjoyed the physical contact that it gave her with men.

Deep down inside she was lonely, and the sorrowful Princess relished the brief moments of attention she would get from sharing an after match bath with the other players.

Phooar!! Is it hot in here or is it just me?

Anyone for a game of hide the soap?

But one day Will's second division TV presenter wife Julia caught the couple emerging from the changing rooms together.

What's going on here?

Nothing dear. Nothing at all. Diana was just leaving.

Oh yeah? Well listen. I've done a fair bit of slapping in my time, and I can tell when something's going on. So just you watch it, Diana!

But despite Will's denials, a special relationship was developing between the Princess and the dashing rugby hero. And as she left, Diana slipped her card into Carling's pocket.

Royal Relief & Majestic Massage
Diana
The Horny Princess
0071 470 240
I'll pamper you in my State Apartments.
Kensington area. All services available.

Continues on page 96.

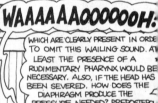

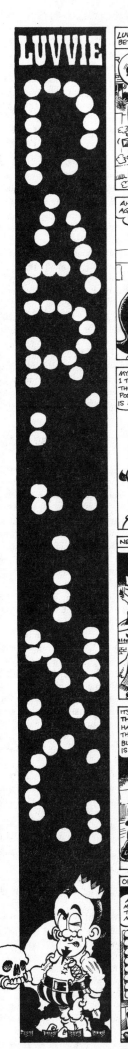

LetterBocks

Big fucker

❑ I'm a student and consequently waste my time (and the tax payer's money) farting around in Europe all summer. It was there on the continent that I spotted this rude bus (right). Do I win £10?
Alexandra Old
Leeds

I spotted this bus in Ireland. A diving special perhaps?

Phil Logie
North Shields

* Typical. You wait 80 issues for a rude bus, then two come at once.

❑ Surely if the budget for 'Stars In Their Eyes' was marginally increased they could hire the original artists to perform their hits badly, instead of getting a bunch of misguided amateur impressionists to do it for them.
Timothy Hamilton-Miller-Smith
London SW18

❑ How do the sceptics who say there's no evidence of the "paranormal" explain these people who frequently "appear" before magistrates? If we can't trust a magistrate, who can we believe?
John Simpson
Weymouth

❑ What a con these Scotch Eggs are. I ate sixteen the other day and didn't feel slightly drunk. I doubt whether there's any whisky in these things at all.
U. Dockrat
Marsworth

❑ Many actors enjoy a comeback in later life after their popularity has appeared to wane. Bette Davis in 'Whatever Happened To Baby Jane?' for example. Or Henry Fonda and Katherine Hepburn in 'On Golden Pond'. How nice to see our own Dame Thora Hird follow in the footsteps of those Hollywood greats by winning a new, young audience with her recent appearance in the Churchill's stair lift advertisement.
K. Cat
Dundee

AS SEEN ON TV

❑ "The least said the soonest mended" or so my grandfather used to say. When my television broke down the other day I decided to follow this advice by ringing the TV repair company and saying nothing. Two months later my television set remains broken and I have heard nothing from the repair company. If nothing else this proves that my grandfather talked bollocks.
H. Rug
Battersea

❑ Here's another late entry for your Viz look-a-like's competition. Mr Logic and Cockney Wanker standing side by side, as seen in our local newspaper.
Mr & Mrs Oosuityousir
Sittingbourne

Convenience foods are a ridiculous idea. Who could possibly be so busy that they have to eat whilst sitting on the lavatory
R.R.
Nottingham

❑ At Eurostar's Waterloo station I spotted a sign saying 'No Trolley's Beyond This Point'. What a splendid marketing idea. I'm sure the sight of girls bending down to pick up their luggage with their fadges on show will encourage more people to use the service.
Surely this little piece of puerile innuendo is worth a fiver?
C. T.
London

THERE'S SOME JIZZ ON THE TITS...
SHE THINKS
IT'S ALL OVER...
EURGH!!
IT IS NOW!

MOTORISTS. Enjoy the freedom of cycling by removing your windscreen, sticking half a melon skin on your head, then jumping red lights and driving the wrong way up one way streets.
Maurice Traveller
Brentford

BEFORE attempting to remove stubborn stains from a garment always circle the stain in permanent marker pen so that when you remove the garment from the washing machine you can easily locate the area of the stain and check that it has gone.
Miss E. Williams
Solihull

GIVE Viz that 'Pulp Fiction' feel by reading the last frames of cartoons first, then reading the rest in a random order.
A. Hulme
Rochdale

TRAFFIC cops. Don't waste time and money installing video cameras in your cars. Install them in the front and rear windows of all Volvo 340s and Maestros driven by old age pensioners. That way all the accidents which the doddering old fogies cause will be recorded on tape.
Andrew Davies
Yarm, Smoggieland

HIGH blood pressure sufferers. Simply cut yourself and bleed for while, thus reducing the pressure in your veins.
N. Rodwell
Herne Bay, Kent

INTERNET users. Save yourself a lot of time and money by simply ringing a public call box and waiting for some sad bastard to walk by with nothing better to do than answer it.
S. Hope
Long Eaton

OLYMPIC athletes. Conceal the fact that you have taken performance enhancing drugs by simply running a little bit slower and letting someone else win.
A. Plasticman
London

TOP TIPS

LORRY drivers. Keep your indicator on for half an hour after each manoeuvre in order to keep us car drivers on our toes.

S. Macreary
Hollingworth

HEAVY smokers. Don't throw away those filters from the end of your cigarettes. Save them up and within a few years you'll have enough to insulate your loft.

Mr J. Hedley
Choppington,
Northumberland

DOG owners. Give passers by the impression that your dog is well trained by ordering it to do whatever it happens to be doing already.

J. Kay
Elem, N.P.

ROAD rage drivers. Settle your dispute honourably by removing your car aerials and having a fencing duel. The aerials will retract if they hit a solid object, thus preventing serious injury.

Pete Doolan
Yeovil

X FILE fans. Create the effect of being abducted by aliens by drinking two bottles of vodka. You'll invariably wake up in a strange place the following morning, having had your memory mysteriously 'erased'.

Sam Neffendorf
Weybridge

CREATE instant designer stubble by sucking a magnet and dipping your chin in a bowl of iron filings.

B. Vilbens
Birmingham

WHEELCHAIR basketball coaches. Miss out Lourdes from any forthcoming European tours in order to avoid losing your star players.

C. Hogg
Hamilton, Lanarkshire

A SHEET of sand paper makes a cheap and effective substitute for costly maps when visiting the Sahara desert.

A. T. Loveday
Ramsgate, Kent

TOBLERONE chocolate bars make ideal 'toast racks' for Ritz crackers.

Max China
Kendal

CAR tyres painted white and wrapped in green tarpaulin sheets make ideal packets of Polos for short sighted giants.

E.F.Gee
Aitchaye

HOUSEWIVES. Brighten up Mondays by coating your kitchen floor with 'Quavers' in order to recreate the sound of walking through virgin snow whilst preparing the tea.

Mrs T.
Thropton

GENTLEMEN. Never smoke a cigar larger than your penis as this may invite witticisms from former partners.

John Butler
Liverpool L17

AVOID drink driving by freezing beer in an ice maker, then eating it.

Urinal Dockrat
Marsworth, Bucks

CELEBRITY CUNTS

We asked Letterbocks readers to nominate stroppy stars for the title of Britain's No.1 celebrity cunt. Here's a few highlights from the cavalcade of cunt nominations which followed.

Carry On Being a Cunt

Kenneth 'Ooh matron' Williams was a right cunt. When I worked in a menswear department in London I had to measure him up for a suit, and he treated me (and everyone else in the shop) like shit.

A.D. Hayes
Maldon, Essex

The biggest celebrity cunt in Buckinghamshire must be Lewis Collins, that roll necked, pouting wanker from 'The Professionals'. He used to frequent the Ivy House pub in Chalfont St. Giles where he had his very own stool at the bar.

Whenever girls came in he'd put on his pout, raise his eyebrows and talk in a deep voice. As if that wasn't bad enough his TV co-star Martin Shaw lived locally too. All we needed was that dead Scottish bloke off the Fine Fare adverts and we'd have had the whole fucking lot of them living in Amersham.

Tango Man
Amersham, Bucks.

❑ Years ago I worked as a scene shifter in the Drury Lane production of Billy Liar. One day, five minutes before curtain up, I was sitting in the crew room having a last cigarette. Sensing another presence I looked up to see the star of the show Michael Crawford adjusting his costume and glaring down at me. "It's a good job some of us are working", he pouted, and then stalked out for his entrance. One minute later the stage manager marched in and fired me - no questions, discussions or excuses. His eventual grudging explanation? "You've upset Michael - he likes everybody standing when he is".
Celebrity cunt? Celebrity *supercunt* more like it.

M. Young
Bristol

❑ I'm that bird who said "Yoo hoo" to Elton John when he was playing tennis in France, and the fat cunt stormed off in a huff and flew home the next day.

That bird
France

* Sorry. That makes him a TWAT as opposed to a cunt.

Needle from Haystack(s)

❑ I posed for this picture with wrestler Giant Haystacks when I was a kid, and he was a proper moany cunt. The flash on my camera took a while to warm up which didn't please the fat bastard one little bit. The resulting picture shows an awe struck 12 year old with what resembles a cross between Terry Hall and a mountain gorilla with 'gland' problems.

James Francis
Rhondda

THE X FLIES

RADIO '96

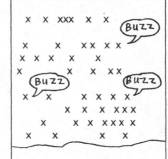

Continued from page 89

Charles celebrated the divorce with a holiday. As in the past, when Charles flew off on holiday he always travelled alone. Like his trip to Scotland a few years previously.

Smoking or non smoking, your Royal Highness?

I want a seat in the cockpit. I feel lucky. I'm going to fly today!

Yes sir, if you say so.

Travelling with their loyal nanny Tiggy 'Legs' Burke was a routine that the children had got used to.

Nenny. Why do ones always travel without ones father?

It's because you're a hair to the throne, William. You can't travel with daddy in case he has an accident.

Meanwhile Charles had a bumpy landing at a Scottish airport...

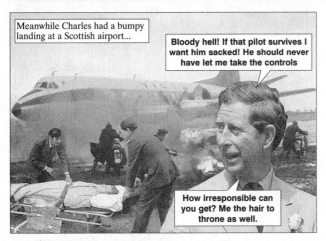

Bloody hell! If that pilot survives I want him sacked! He should never have let me take the controls

How irresponsible can you get? Me the hair to throne as well.

Waaaah!!

At times Charles had lead a charmed life. During the eighties he narrowly escaped death in a sledging accident at the swish holiday resort of Cloisters. A close friend was killed in the accident.

Anyway, getting back to the story...

After the divorce Diana took a much needed holiday, but her life seemed empty and without purpose.

Now living alone in a tiny Palace, even her closest friends began to dessert her.

Hello Will. How's things?

Oh, not too bad. Wife's left me, and my career's on the blink. I just came round to say goodbye really. It was fun knowing you when you were a Princess... but erm... Mrs Wales doesn't really sound the same does it?

Diana had never felt so alone. Not even in the past when she'd felt really alone on previous occasions. Alone and unloved, she cried herself to sleep.

The next morning she decided to throw herself into her charity work...

And this is your leg is it?

Yes, that's right.

It's black. Is it supposed to be that colour?

Yes, it is.

Hello. And what's your name?

Hello. And what's your name?

Hello. And what's your name?

Hello. And what's your name?

And what's your name?

Oh God!

Harry, remember? I'm your son.

Continues on page 104

Ready, steady, GHOST!

THE Paranormal Olympic Games are to be held in Limbo in the year 2002.

Within hours of the announcement shops and businesses in the state, which exists somewhere between Heaven and Hell, were looking forward to the prospect of an economic boom which the money spinning spirit games will guarantee.

Souls

Over five million souls are expected to watch the games, in which ghosts, poltergeists and other supernatural entities from all over the world compete for medals. Events include the severed head put, wall walking, chain dragging and the 100 metre lurch through a cemetary. An estimated 80 million spirits around the world will watch the events telepathically.

Limbo

Limbo's success comes as a blow to Shangri La which had been confident of hosting the prestigious event for the first time. Limbo has already staged the games once, in 1968, and that occasion Russia were accused of cheating after murdering several of their top athletes and not allowing their souls to rest in order to gain qualification to the event.

Samba

Geographical disadvantages are thought to have swayed the Committee's final decision. Shangri La -

a wonderful place of true perfection - would have proven popular among spectators and athletes alike. But there would have been problems with transport. Thought to be in Nepal, the only way to get to Shangri La is by climbing through high mountains. According to legend an avalanche then occurs and an icy cave appears leading to the mythical place.

Lambada

Other disappointed delegations included representatives of Nirvana, the state of utter bliss where people no longer require their bodies. Olympic chiefs feared that out-of-body competitions would reduce the incentive for athletes to train. Photo finishes would also have been difficult to decide.

Lumbago

Eldorado, with its slogan 'the lost city of gold', had been favourites among the early bidders. Its high profile campaign to host the games was supported by many big names including W.G. Grace, Charlie Chaplin and Martin Luther King. However its whereabouts are unknown and the Committee was unable to visit it to check the facilities on offer. Disappointed Norwegian delegates from Valhalla were already talking opti-

Ghosts going for ghould, shiver and bronzergeist in paranormal games

An American head putter makes a spooky spectre as he ghouls for gold at the 1998 Paranormal Olympics in Hades

mistically about their chances of staging the 2006 games. Facilities in the mythical Hall of the Viking Kings are second to none. However problems over qualification for events have yet to be resolved. As the legends stand only athletes who died in battle with a sword in their hand could qualify for the final stages in the mythical Hall itself.

The Committee were keen to avoid any such problems, particularly in the wake of the 1994 fiasco in Hades, the Greek Hell, where competitors were forced to queue for hours with coins in their mouths waiting for a ferryman to take them across the river Styx. Many turned up late for their events and were disqualified as a result.

DOCTOR, I'VE GOT A STIFF BACK

RETURN TO SENDER

QUEEN BUM!

Her Royal Lowness is a crown and out

ONCE she was the Queen of England. Bedecked in jewels and dressed in lavish gowns, red carpets unfurled beneath her every foot. But now she wanders alone in a public park, huddled in rags, her only companion a mangey dog.

Runcible

There was a time when she lived a life of luxury and splendour, dining on swans and caviar, and slices of quince which she ate with a runcible spoon. Crowds flocked in their thousands to see her changing the guards at Buckingham Palace. But nowadays she prefers liquidised vegetable soup, and even her relatives avoid her as the Queen Mother seldom changes her clothing. In her heyday she was everyone's favourite Royal. But now she whiles away the hours at the Clarence House care home in central London, just another muddled pensioner waiting for the grave.

Crucible

Neighbours of the 98 year old fear for the health of the former Queen. She can often be seen wandering aimlessly in the local parks, and has trouble remembering who she is. On one occasion she was found singing in a bus shelter and told police officers she was Gracie Fields. Police and park wardens regularly round the old dear up and hand her back to nursing home staff. A Buckingham Palace source yesterday denied the Queen Mother was suffering from Alzheimer's disease or any similar marble mislaying illness.

Pensioner's nightmare ends in amputation

CONSUMER watchdogs are warning old folk to be on their guard after a frail Yorkshire pensioner allowed artificial leg salesmen to cut off both of his legs.

Eighty-six year old Wilfred Barker - a veteran of two world wars - was subjected to over ten hours of high pressure sales pitching after two men turned up uninvited at his Barnsley home at 2 o'clock in the morning.

Raining

"I invited them in because it was raining and made them a cup of tea. After a while, when I realised they were selling legs, I told them I'd already got some. But they said there was no obligation for me to buy and they just wanted to give me a quick demonstration".

Pouring

The two salesmen from Leeds based Alpine Legs then produced impressive, glossy, brochures showing photographs of several attractive new artificial limbs. But when they began quoting prices Wilfred told them straight away that he wasn't interested.

Snoring

"They measured my legs and came up with a price of over £10,000. I don't have that sort of money. Then they started telling me how much it was going to cost just to maintain my real legs. They said my old legs were coming to the end of their life and it wasn't worth having them repaired. I'd be better off investing in a new pair. I got a bit bamboozled. Then, after a while it seemed to make sense".

Bed

Mr Barker asked the salesmen for time to think, and suggested they return the following day. But they told him they were only in the area for one night and that this was a special offer. "They said if I didn't sign there and then the price would be doubled, and I might end up with no legs at all".

Head

Their aggressive sales pitch continued until dawn

Leg salesmen got their feet in the door

and throughout the ordeal they refused to allow Mr Barker to use the lavatory. He pleaded with them to leave, but they said they would only go if he allowed them to cut off his legs. At around noon the following day, exhausted and suffering from bladder cramps, Wilfred eventually agreed.

Morning

"They put a piece of paper in front of me and told me that if I signed it they would go away and let me sleep. So I did. Before I knew what was happening they'd sawn my legs off above the knee."

Cash

Wilfred handed over £4,500 cash on the spot. The men then left, promising to return the next day to fit his replacement legs. But he heard nothing for over six weeks. Then he received another bill, this time for £24,000. "The first payment had only been a deposit, and they were refusing to fit my new legs until I paid the balance."

Mathis

Reluctantly Mr Barker sold his house in order to pay the bill. Two weeks later two men arrived and fitted his new legs, breaking his hip and two ribs in the process. "They were only here a couple of minutes but I couldn't believe the mess they made". Since then Wilfred has had nothing but trouble from his new legs. "The left one is too short and rattles when I go ballroom dancing. The other one just keeps falling off. I feel such a fool".

Morris

When we showed Wilfred's legs to a leading orthopaedic surgeon he

Mr Barker with the two unevenly lengthed walking sticks he now needs to stand up.

was horrified.
"This is a really shoddy job. For a start Mr Barker's legs haven't been sawn off evenly. And even worse, he's been fitted with two left legs. They've not been weatherproofed properly and water is already ingressing and causing swelling of the knees", he added.

Austin

A spokesman for OffPeg, the regulatory body responsible for artificial limbs and appliances have issued a warning to any old folk who were thinking of buying replacement legs. "Shop around, go to a reputable company or ask friends who've had their legs sawn off successfully and are happy with their replacements", he said. "But most importantly, never sign anything on the doorstep. Always ask for time to consider. Unless of course there's a special offer you might miss".

Wolsley

Meanwhile Alpine Legs managing director Reg Shit flatly denied that his employees use any high pressure sales techniques. "All my salesmen are nice blokes. In fact the gentleman concerned used to be vicar. As far as I'm aware Mr Barker's legs fit perfectly well. Now fuck off out of it or I'll set me dog on you", he told us.

GILBERT RATCHET'S FANTASTIC VOYAGE

I'M REALLY EXCITED, READERS - I'M TAKING PART IN A REMARKABLE SCIENTIFIC EXPERIMENT TODAY...

..I'M GOING TO BE SHRUNK DOWN TO MINISCULE SIZE BY THIS ELECTRONIC MINIATURISING RAY GUN, AND THEN INJECTED INTO GLENDA JACKSON'S BLOODSTREAM...

...IN ORDER TO RAISE MONEY FOR CHARITY

SO

ACTIVATE THE MINIATURISING RAY!

BZZZZ

MINIATURISING RAY ACTIVATED!

NOW THEN. WE CAREFULLY PLACE THE MINIATURISED GILBERT INTO THIS SYRINGE...

...AND PREPARE TO INJECT HIM INTO GLENDA JACKSON'S BLOODSTREAM

READY WHEN YOU ARE, MR SCIENTIST

GILBERT'S VOICE

WOW! THIS IS ABSOLUTELY AMAZING

...I'M ACTUALLY INSIDE THE VEIN OF THE FAMOUS ACTRESS-TURNED-LABOUR MP GLENDA JACKSON!

SHORTLY

OH DEAR. MY CAT HAS GOT TRAPPED UP IN GLENDA JACKSON'S RIBCAGE...

...HOW ON EARTH SHALL I GET HIM DOWN?

NEVER FEAR! I'LL SAVE YOUR LITTLE KITTY —

...WITH THE AID OF MY TRUSTY HAMMER

CRUNCH

THERE NOW. THE ENORMOUS COMEDY BUMP WHICH HAS SPROUTED FROM YOUR HEAD CAN BE USED AS A "FIREMAN'S POLE" FOR YOUR CAT TO SLIDE DOWN TO SAFETY

THANK YOU YOUNG MAN

COR! THERE'S A WOMEN'S INSTITUTE CHARITY BAZAAR BEING HELD IN GLENDA JACKSON'S DUODENUM. BRILLIANT!

WI CHARITY BAZAAR
12 NOON TODAY
GLENDA JACKSON'S DUODENUM
5P ADMISSION

TROUBLE IS, IT COSTS FIVE PEE ADMISSION - AND I'M SKINT AGAIN

WHAT'S WRONG MR MAYOR - YOU LOOK A BIT FED UP

I'M SUPPOSED TO BE OPENING THIS NEW CHILDRENS' WARD IN GLENDA JACKSON'S BRONCHIAL TUBES...

CHILDREN'S

BUT I CAN'T CUT THE RIBBON BECAUSE MY FINGERS ARE TOO FAT TO FIT THE SCISSORS PROPERLY

A SPOT OF DIY LIPOSUCTION WITH THIS VACUUM CLEANER WILL SLIM DOWN YOUR PODGY FINGERS

ALL I ASK IN RETURN IS A FIVE PENCE REWARD

WHOOPS! I'D ACCIDENTLY SET THE VACUUM CLEANER TO 'BLOW'

BLOOT

YOU BLITHERING OAF. NOW MY FINGERS ARE FATTER THAN EVER

IF YOU THINK YOU'RE GETTING FIVE PEE OUT OF ME, YOU CAN FUCK OFF

DRAT! I'M A KEEN BIRD WATCHER BUT GLENDA JACKSON'S GALL BLADDER IS NOTABLE FOR IT'S TOTAL ABSENCE OF ANY FEATHERED FRIENDS WHATSOEVER

BY COVERING MYSELF WITH FEATHERS AND RUNNING AROUND LIKE A TWAT, I CAN PROVIDE YOU WITH A CONVINCING ORNITHOLOGICAL EXTRAVAGANZA FOR SEVERAL HOURS

GREAT!

TWEET TWITTER

THANKS GILBERT. HERE'S ONE THOUSAND POUNDS AND FIVE PENCE

SO, IN GLENDA JACKSON'S DUODENUM

HOORAY. NOW I CAN AFFORD TO GET INTO THE WOMEN'S INSTITUTE CHARITY BAZAAR AND BUY A GRAND'S WORTH OF HOME-MADE CHUTNEY WHILE I'M THERE

W.I. CHARITY BA
CAKES - CHUTNEY - SOFT TOYS - FRIGGING HAND WOVEN TABLEMATS

AFTER 15 PINTS

What was the round?

BECOMES IT DIFFICULT BAR TO GET THE TO

After 5 pints your speech becomes slurred. After 10 pints your vision becomes cloudy. After 15 pints your legs go all wobbly. How then does a Royal marine Commando get back to his barracks?

Easy. He's been thoroughly trained to cope with the situation in the first place, by drinking to excess on a regular basis. Do you think you could cope?

In the absence of a real pub, read through these questions. There aren't necessarily right or wrong answers, but your answers must be completely honest. We need pissheads, but they must be total pissheads.

After a hard day of exercises your unit returns to base. You've got the evening off. What do you do?
a) Clean your kit, polish your boots, and get an early nights kip.
b) Go to the mess, play cards or watch TV with your mates.
c) March straight off to the pub, mob handed, for a night on the piss.

followed by "... pints of lager". Now, without looking at your cigarette packet, how many fags have you got left?

Drinking with the Royal Marines you need to pay attention to detail and remember even small things which at first seem unimportant. It's not just about drinking. It's about thinking too.

How well you can tell the time without looking at your watch? Shout out loud what time last orders is. Now look at your watch. How many minutes are there left till closing time? How many pints can you drink in that time? Whose round is it next?

You've had ten pints and you need a piss, but the toilets are 12 metres away across a crowded room. What do you do?

a) Stagger across the room to the toilets, leering at women on your way

b) Finish your pint then piss in the glass
c) Finish your pint, piss in the glass and then drink the contents whilst standing on a table

Next a mammary test. Look at these tits. Nudge the person next to you and say "Phooarr!" out loud.

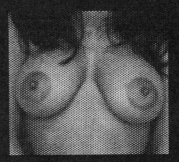

On operations and in training exercises Marines often have to form a plan where none exists. Imagine for a moment eight of you are out on a crawl and you arrive at a pub with only enough drinking time left for one round. But there's

another pub just 300 yards down the road. Time is against you so you need to think quickly. What do you do?

a) Relax and enjoy your last drink where you are.
b) Knock back your pints as quickly as possible, then leg it to the next pub.
c) Send one man ahead to the next pub to line up a double round on the bar, while the other seven drink two pints each in the first pub before going on to join him.

On your way back to barracks you pass a chip shop. You fancy some chips, but you feel dizzy and sick. What do you do?

a) Forget the chips, and head straight home.
b) Make yourself puke on the doorstep, then go in and order some chips.
c) Go in and pick a fight with the first civvy you spot standing in the queue, and put him in hospital.

The fact you've bothered to read this far already says a lot about you. It says you're bored, and you've got fuck all better to do. You might well be the sort of person we're looking for.

But you'll have to prove yourself. Our training is intense and hard - Stag night conditions every night. You'll learn advanced drinking techniques. But its not just about how much you can drink - its about what you can handle afterwards. A curry, a fight, and a five mile hike back to barracks.

One final question. What's the first thing that springs to mind when you look at this picture of a cracker biscuit?

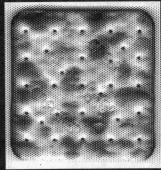

If the answer is wank on it, we'd like to hear from you.

It's your round. Wherever you are, turn around quickly and scan the room, then turn back. How many people did you see behind you? Shout the number out loud,

SEMPER FIGHTUM INEBRIATAE et

ROYAL MARINE COMMANDOS

Continued from page 97

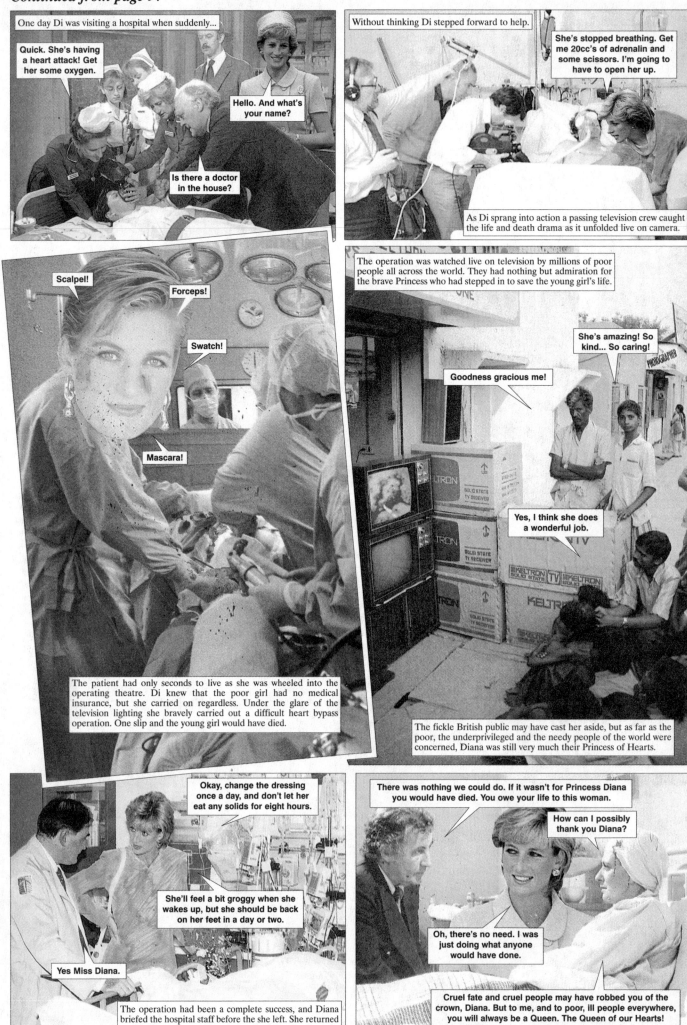

The End

WONDERWARM!

Rory blows valve on heating

Four letter Oasis star Liam Gallagher has spoken out for the first time about the central heating system that keeps him warm in winter.

The outrageous billionaire drug crazed spitting singer has been holed up in a country hideaway with leggy lovebomb Patsy Kensit since returning from the band's disastrous US tour.

Remote

We tracked the couple down to a remote £10 million, 8 bedroom farmhouse in the Sussex countryside. The house, which stands in its own garden, is heated by a traditional sealed circulating hot water system. It has plentiful radiators to the ground and first floors, plus electric night storage heaters in two attic bedrooms.

Radio

Liam revealed for the first time the truth about the cost of heating the house. "It costs a fortune to heat, but who cares? I'm fucking loaded". The foul mouthed star told us the heating ran on LPG, or liquid petroleum gas.

Out of

Inside the house Liam showed us into a utility room where a combination boiler was mounted

Writes our Pop & Plumbing Correspondent
the late boozed up wiggy newsreader
REGINALD BOSANQUET

on a bare brick wall. A timer switch nearby allowed the controversial rocker and his blonde fiancee to preset the heating to come and off at certain times of the day.
A booster switch enables Gallagher and his stunning bride-to-be to over-ride these preset times if required, making hot water available at short notice any time of the day or night.

Upstairs

In an upstairs bathroom we saw a double panel radiator with towel rail above, while in a cupboard nearby stood a well lagged hot water tank.

Downstairs

Locals at the nearby Kings Head pub told us that natural gas is not available in the area and the only alternative fuel to LPG would be oil. "Propane gas used to be cheaper than oil, but political unrest in the Middle East has caused prices to soar in recent years", said landlord Jack Higgins.

Oasis gas-fired secrets exposed

CHAMPAGNE SUPERBOILER:
Liam makes an obscene gesture next to the couple's 'Valiant' wall mounted combination boiler.

WHAT'S THE STORY? BATHROOM RADIATOR:
Patsy poses alongside the couple's double panel fluted bathroom radiator. Their towel rail is just out of shot.

RORY GALLAGHER, the unknown brother of Oasis twins Niall and Liam has written a 'plumb and tell' book pulling the plug on the family's childhood heating arrangements.

Duchess

Sick of seeing lies about his family printed in the press, younger brother Rory has decided to pipe up and set the record straight. And he reveals that contrary to some reports, the Gallagher family did **NOT** have Economy 7 night storage heating. "We didn't have any central heating in those days", he told us yesterday. "Just coal fires, and one paraffin heater which we kept in the bathroom".

Duke St.

Coal fires were once the standard form of domestic heating in British households. Nowadays restrictions on the use of solid fuel would mean the Gallagher triplets having to buy smokeless coal 'brickettes' were they to light a fire in certain areas.

DRUNKEN DAD HIT KIDS WITH POKER

THE Gallagher's drunken father Hughie regularly branded his kids with a red hot fireside poker, younger brother Rory has revealed.

"He kept a set of partly ornamental tools, including a fork, a small shovel and some tongs on the hearth", he told us yesterday. "The shovel was of little practical use because the handle became loose and unscrewed itself whenever it was used".

Millionaire twins Liam and Nigel gave their drunken father away to a jumble sale in 1988. He is currently in prison for swearing at a Sun photographer who poked him repeatedly with a sharp stick.

Hughie Gallagher yesterday

DON'T LOOK BACK AT THE WATER TANK:
Liam's cosy hot water tank complete with foam insulation.

Raffles The Gentleman Thug

GOSH, RAFFLES - I'M SO EXCITED! PLAYING AT LORD'S!

YES, BUNNY. GENTLEMEN VERSUS M.C.C. IN AID OF QUEEN ALEXANDREA'S CRIMEAN RELIEF FUND.

SHAME YOU DIDN'T THINK TO BOOK SEATS, RAFFLES OLD CHAP.

NO NEED. THIS IS THE ONLY RESERVATION I NEED.

PHEEP!

MY SEAT, I BELIEVE SIR.

NO SIR. I FEAR YOU MUST BE MISTAKEN, FOR I PROCURED MY RESERVATION FROM THE CLERK OF THE BOOKING OFFICE SOME THREE WEEKS AGO.

I'M SORRY?

MIGHT I POLITELY ENQUIRE SIR, IF YOU ARE PERHAPS A TAD HARD OF HEARING OR WHAT?

WOULD YOU PLEASE BE SO GOOD AS TO KINDLY WATCH MY FUCKING LIPS. MY SEAT. OUT.

WELL... I... I SHALL SPEAK TO THE GUARD ABOUT THIS...

THIS IS AN OUTRAGE SIR!

FOR ALL THAT I AM CONCERNED ABOUT YOUR OPINIONS, SIR, YOU MAY TAKE A FLYING FUCK AT A ROLLING DOUGHNUT.

I SAY SIR. LOOK AT THIS CHARMING YOUNG FILLY. AS SPLENDID AN EMBONPOINT AS I HAVE SEEN - AND A FINELY TURNED BRACE OF ANKLES, WHAT?

I'LL WAGER SHE GOES LIKE A NECESSARIUM DOOR IN A NOT INCONSIDERABLY SEVERE GALE. LOOK - IN THIS GRAVURE YOU CAN NEARLY SEE HER MINGEPIECE.

GREAT SCOTT! WHAT CRACKING BEEF CURTAINS! SINGULARLY FORMIDABLE, WHAT?

DO YOU MIND SIR? THERE ARE LADIES PRESENT IN THIS COMPARTMENT. PLEASE DESIST WITH YOUR BAWDY CHARNEL-HOUSE BANTER.

I'M SORRY MY GOOD FELLOW. WERE YOU ADDRESSING ME, OR PERCHANCE MASTICATING ON A HOUSE-BRICK?

ERM... I DON'T QUITE...

...BECAUSE ONE LOSES ONE'S FUCKING TEETH BOTH WAYS UP.

CLOCK!

MARYLEBONE, RAFFLES! OUR STOP!

GOOD DAY TO YOU.

AT LORD'S...

EGAD! LOOK, RAFFLES OLD BEAN! IT'S DR. W.G. GRACE! I'VE READ SO MUCH ABOUT HIM IN THE SPORTING PAGES OF THE LONDON TIMES!

IN THE CHANGING ROOMS...

EXCUSE ME BUNNY OLD CHAP. I MUST JUST ANSWER A CALL OF NATURE.

Button Bunion

GOOD AFTERNOON TO YOU, SIR.

IF I MAY MAKE SO BOLD SIR - WHAT ARE YOU LOOKING AT?

NOTHING SIR, NOTHING AT ALL.

ARE YOU CALLING MY COCK NOTHING?

LATER...

HOWZAT SIR?

OUT.

I SAY RAFFLES OLD CHAP - WHAT A TOPPING OFF-BREAK! W.G. GRACE IS NEXT IN TO BAT!

OOH... ME HEAD... WHERE AM I...?

Doctor POOLITTLE

HE TALKS TO THE ANIMALS — about constipation

DAMN! DAMN! DAMN! AND BLAST!

LANGUAGE DOCTOR!

OH BUT CONFOUND IT MRS. H.! IT'S NEARLY THREE WEEKS SINCE I MOVED MY BOWELS!

OH DEAR DEAR DOCTOR, DON'T WORRY, I'M SURE YOU'LL DO A WEE JOBBY SOON.

YES. I'LL GO FOR A RIDE ON MY PENNY FARTHING AND SEE IF I CAN SHAKE IT DOWN.

SHORTLY...

I SAY! LOOK AT THAT PILE OF ORDURE!... WHY IS IT THAT THE BEASTS OF THE ZOO FIND IT SO EASY TO EVACUATE THEIR BOWELS?

WHY CAN'T I DO THAT? IF ONLY I HAD THEIR SECRET.

... IF I COULD ONLY **TALK** TO THEM...

IF I COULD TALK TO THE ANIMALS, LEARN THEIR LANGUAGES, HOW UN-CONSTI-PATED LIFE WOULD BE.

IF I COULD BANTER OVER FAECES, WITH A MYRIAD OF SPECIES, I'D UNLOAD MY BREAKFAST LUNCH AND TEA.

I WOULD MUSE ABOUT SLOPPY TURDS, WITH A FLOCK OF BIRDS, TAKE ADVICE ON LAXATIVES FROM OWLS.

I'D ASK HORSES IN THE STABLE, HOW THEY'D LAY A CABLE, WITH THEIR ADVICE I'D GO AND MOVE MY BOWELS.

I'D HAVE A CHAT A-BOUT SHITTING WITH AN OCELOT...

I'D ASK AN OSTRICH HOW IT PARKS IT'S FUDGE...

... AND IF YOU ASK ME WHY I STRAIN MY BOT-A-LOT, I'D SAY MY CHOC-O-LOT...

WON'T BUDGE!

IF I COULD SHIT LIKE THE MONKEYS DO, RIGHT HERE IN THE ZOO, THROTTLING A MARS BAR UP A TREE.

I WOULD CHATTER WITH A PARROT, ABOUT STRANGLING A CARROT, WHAT A TOPPING DROPPING THAT WOULD BE.

IF I COULD JUST ASK A PRAIRIE DOG, HOW HE DROPS A LOG, PONDER OVER SENNA PODS WITH ANTS.

IF I COULD **WALK** WITH THE ANIMALS...

...TALK WITH THE ANIMALS...

LION'S CAGE

... GRUNT AND SQUEAK AND SQUALK WITH THE ANIMALS.

ROOOAARGH!!

OH FUCK, I'VE SHIT MY PANTS.

THE CRITICS

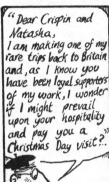

Review: 101 DALMATIONS
In spite of references to the Croatian refugees in the title, this film is, in fact, a noiresque pastiche of Jacobean revenge tragedy, which raises deep questions concerning the Freudian quest for animal identity through possession of skin. The recurring Orwellian '101' motif leads one to

WELL, THAT'S MY LAST REVIEW OF THE YEAR FAXED OFF TO THE GUARDIAN... I'M ON HOLIDAY!

ME TOO!

WHIRRRRR

HOW ONE *RELISHES* A FEW QUIET DAYS AWAY FROM THE *SYCOPHANTIC FAWNING* WHICH PERVADES THE WORLD OF THE ARTS...

INDEED... NOW LET'S SEE WHAT THE POST HAS BROUGHT...

TSK! ANOTHER *REVOLTINGLY SENTIMENTAL* CARD... SOME OF OUR FRIENDS HAVE NO SENSE OF AESTHETICS...

WOW!!

WHAT IS IT?

IT'S A LETTER FROM SIR PETER BROOKE-GROANAWAY, THE FILM AUTEUR, ART CONNOISSEUR AND INTERNATIONAL THEATRE DIRECTOR...

SIR PETER?! WRITING TO US?!

"Dear Crispin and Natasha,
I am making one of my rare trips back to Britain and, as I know you have been loyal supporters of my work, I wonder if I might prevail upon your hospitality and pay you a Christmas Day visit?.."

ONE IS *OVERWHELMED* BY THE PROSPECT OF RECEIVING SUCH A *COLOSSAL GENIUS* INTO ONE'S HUMBLE HOME!

WE MUST ENSURE THAT OUR HOUSE IS *AESTHETICALLY WORTHY* OF HIS PRESENCE..

A day later....

RIGHT, WE'VE CREATED A PURE UNCLUTTERED SPACE....

MAYBE JUST A FEW BOOKS, RANDOMLY SELECTED FROM OUR COLLECTION...

LET'S COMMISSION SOME NEW WORKS OF ART FROM A DARING YOUNG ARTIST.

OH *YES!* I'M SURE SIR PETER WILL BE IMPRESSED THAT WE'RE BRINGING A STRUGGLING YOUNG TALENT INTO AN ALL TOO CLIQUEY ART MARKET...

HI, AUNT NATASHA.

GOOD OF YOU TO TAKE ON THIS COMMISSION, DAMIEN.

WE THOUGHT PERHAPS YOU MIGHT CREATE SOME PIECES AROUND A CHRISTMAS THEME..

...SUBVERT SOCIETY'S PRECONCEPTIONS OF THE LOW-ART STATUS OF SEASONAL DECORATION...

NAH PROBS...JUS' GIVE US THE CHEQUE AN I'LL SORT YOU SOMEFING AHT, AWRIGHT?

£100,000 ARTS COUNCIL

Later....

FOUGHT I'D START IN THIS ROOM...

A CHRISTMAS TREE!...ER..WE HAD SOMETHING RATHER MORE.. ER.. *RADICAL* IN MIND...

NAH, NAH! I'M NOT GONNA PUT IT UP!... I'M USIN' THE NEEDLES TO DO A *WORD-ART FLOOR - INSTALLATION* SEE?

SHAKE

SPRINKLE

DAMIEN FORGES THE VERY SUBSTANCE OF NATURE ITSELF INTO AN ODE TO THE SAVAGE BEAUTY OF WINTER....

FUCK ART IT'S CHRISTMAS

NOW, HOW ABOUT AN INSTALLATION IN THE LIVING ROOM?

YEAH, I GOT AN IDEA FOR THAT... HAD TO SEND OFF TO LAPLAND FOR THE MATERIALS...

SURELY BRITISH ART HAS FOUND ITS NEW *ENFANT TERRIBLE*...

FORMALDEHYDE

Christmas Day....

SIR PETER WILL BE HERE AT ANY MOMENT... LOOK, I'VE FOUND SOME *EASTERN EUROPEAN* ANIMATION ON VIDEO TO WATCH, INSTEAD OF ALL THOSE SHALLOW BRITISH *CARTOONS* THEY SHOW AT CHRISTMAS...

FANCY SOME CHEESE GROMOVICH?

WALLSKY AND GROMOVICH

THE LUNCH IS NEARLY READY... I'M SURE SIR PETER WON'T WANT TO *CONTAMINATE* HIS PALATE WITH THE BLAND STODGE WHICH PASSES FOR COOKING IN THIS COUNTRY...

...SO WE'RE HAVING A ROULADE OF QUAIL'S FOOT PÂTÉ AND OAK-SMOKED GARLIC, ENFOLDED IN A CHOCOLATE AND CORIANDER SAUCE, SERVED ON A FUTON OF LIGHTLY SAUTEED WILD RICE FOLLOWED BY A...

RRING! RRING!

CRISPIN?...PETER HERE. ...AFRAID I'LL BE A BIT LATE... AS I WAS DRIVING ACROSS LONDON I FELT MOVED TO STOP AND TAKE IN ALL THE WONDERFUL CHRISTMAS LIGHTS... ...QUITE OVERCOME!..

PHONE BOX

HA HA! WHAT A WONDERFUL SENSE OF *IRONY* YOU HAVE SIR PETER!... I'M SURE THE *HIDEOUSLY KITSCH* TAT WHICH DEFACES OUR CAPITAL'S ARCHITECTURE IS *UNBEARABLY OFFENSIVE* TO YOUR SENSITIVE EYE..

NOT AT ALL! I *LOVE* IT!

I *LOVE* THE SIMPLE PROLETARIAN *UNPRETENTIOUSNESS* OF THE TRADITIONAL BRITISH CHRISTMAS... THE *NAÏVE* CARDS, THE TACKY TREES, THE PROPER TURKEY DINNER...

An hour later...

WELL, I'VE STUCK MOST OF THE NEEDLES BACK ONTO THE TREE AND PUT THE CARDS BACK UP BUT WE'LL NEVER GET A TURKEY AT THIS SHORT NOTICE!

HMM...

MARVELLOUS!... I MUST SAY, THAT'S THE BIGGEST TURKEY I'VE EVER SEEN!

Victorian-style mock-holly ivy

John Fardell '96

ROGER MELLIE - THE MAN ON THE TELLY

BOLLOCKS!

ROGER AND TOM ARE HAVING A QUIET DRINK IN HARPO'S, THE TRENDY SOHO WATERING HOLE...

WHO'D HAVE THOUGHT IT?..ME, ROGER MELLIE, APPEARING ON 'THIS IS YOUR LIFE'

IT WAS SUCH A SHOCK. I REALLY HAD NO IDEA THEY WERE GOING TO SPRING IT ON ME LIKE THAT, TOM. I REALLY DIDN'T

PEAK TIME T.V. SHOULD BE QUITE A BOOST FOR MY CAREER, EH?

I DON'T KNOW, ROGER...

THE PAPERS ARE GIVING THE SHOW MIXED REVIEWS

OH, FUCKING HELL! THEY'RE NOT DREDGING UP THAT WIFE SLAPPING SHIT AGAIN, ARE THEY?

TV SHAME OF WIFE BEATER MELLIE

THAT WAS PERSONAL! IT SHOULD NEVER HAVE BEEN REVEALED ON THE PROGRAMME

REVEALED ON THE PROGRAMME!?!... BUT ROGER...YOU DID IT LIVE ON THE PROGRAMME

YOU WOULD HAVE KILLED HER IF MICHAEL ASPEL HADN'T PULLED YOU OFF AND GOT YOU IN A HALF NELSON

DON'T BE RIDICULOUS, TOM. I KNOW WHEN TO STOP. BUT SPARE THE ROD AND SPOIL THE WIFE. A GOOD GAZZERING ONCE IN A WHILE LET'S 'EM KNOW WHO'S BOSS

LEAVING ASIDE THE SEX-UAL POLITICS, ROGER, YOU MUST ADMIT, HITTING YOUR WIFE ON LIVE T.V. CREATES A BIT OF A P.R. PROBLEM

PROBLEM!?! WHAT PROBLEM? I APOLOGISED, DIDN'T I?

NO, ROGER. THAT'S NOT THE POINT

WE NEED TO PAPER OVER THE CRACKS A LITTLE...REPAIR THE DAMAGE I'D LIKE YOU TO MEET SOMEONE

IN THE BISTRO... ROGER...THIS IS EUGEN LAGER. HE'S A P.R. GURU AND HE'S JUST THE MAN TO HELP YOU REBUILD YOUR CARING, FAMILY MAN IMAGE

HI, ROGER. WON'T YOU JOIN ME FOR A MOZORRELLA SANDWICH?

SO WHAT WE NEED TO DO IS PRESENT A UNITED FRONT. PICTURES OF YOU AND THE WIFE AT HOME, WALKING THE DOG, DOMESTIC BLISS, SMILES ALL ROUND

SOUNDS GOOD, EH, ROGER?

I'VE SPOKEN TO THE EDITOR OF 'HIYA' MAGAZINE AND SHE'S KEEN TO DO AN 'AT HOME' FEATURE. SHOTS OF YOUR BEAUTIFUL HOME. YOU AND THE WIFE RELAXING BY THE FIRE, ALL THAT STUFF

TOM WILL BRING THEIR CAMERAMAN TO YOUR HOUSE AT TEN TOMORROW. MAKE SURE THINGS ARE SPICK AND SPAN, EH?

DON'T WORRY. EVERYTHING WILL BE HUNKY DORY. I'LL GET THE PIG TO PUSH THE HOOVER AROUND FOR AN HOUR BEFORE I GET UP.

THE NEXT MORNING, TOM AND THE PHOTOGRAPHER ARRIVE ON TIME...

ROGER LOVES GARDENING

HMMM!!

HE AND MARY SPEND A LOT OF TIME TOGETHER IN THE GARDEN

AH, ROGER. THIS IS FABIAN, FROM 'HIYA' MAGAZINE

ERM, CAN I HAVE A QUICK WORD, TOM... IN PRIVATE

INSIDE... ROGER. DON'T BE SO RUDE. YOU'VE CLOSED THE DOOR IN HIS FACE. WHAT'S GOING ON?

BIT OF A PROBLEM ON THE 'UNITED FRONT' FRONT, TOM

SHE HASN'T LEFT YOU, HAS SHE?

WELL, IN A SENSE, SHE HAS, YES

SHE'S HERE, BUT THEN AGAIN, SHE ISN'T

WHAT DO YOU MEAN?

I'VE TOPPED HER, TOM. SHE'S DEAD!

JESUS CHRIST! I DON'T BELIEVE IT!

ROGER...HOW ON EARTH COULD YOU?!?

IT WAS HER FAULT, TOM. SHE WAS RUBBISHING MY FAMILY

SAID I HAD A BAD TEMPER ...AND I JUST SNAPPED!

BUT DON'T PANIC, TOM. I'VE BEEN THINKING ON MY FEET. WE'LL DO THE PICTURES WITHOUT HER. TELL THEM SHE'S GOT A HEADACHE. STICK HER IN BED, PRETEND SHE'S ASLEEP OR SOMETHING

OH, GOD...I DON'T BELIEVE THIS IS HAPPENING

HELLO. SORRY TO INTERRUPT, BUT IS IT OKAY IF I START SETTING...

...UP MY GEAR?

AAAAAGH!!!

OOPS!

OKAY, TOM. HERE'S PLAN B. I'VE GOT MY WHITE RANGE ROVER OUT THE BACK

MURDER! MURDER!

WE JUMP IN IT, DRIVE AROUND FOR A BIT AND... ERM... THAT'LL GIVE ME TIME TO THINK!

WE INTERRUPT THIS PROGRAMME TO BRING YOU NEWS OF A DRAMATIC STORY UNFOLDING LIVE! MARY MELLIE, WIFE OF T.V. PRESENTER ROGER, HAS BEEN MURDERED. WE NOW GO OVER LIVE TO THE F.T.V. NEWS HELICOPTER...

AND BELOW US WE SEE THE WHITE RANGE ROVER DRIVEN BY T.V. HOST ROGER MELLIE, BEING FOLLOWED BY SIX POLICE CARS. WE BELIEVE HE IS ARMED AND IS REFUSING TO STOP.

DON'T YOU THINK THIS IS GETTING A BIT OUT OF HAND, ROGER?

DON'T WORRY, TOM. I'M A PRO. I CAN HANDLE A BIT OF PRESSURE

IT'S ALL A STORM IN A TEA CUP. WE'LL JUST DRIVE ROUND FOR A BIT TILL THINGS COOL DOWN...

Don't miss the trial of R.J.Mellie - LIVE in the next issue!

Are you a PIMP or a SCIENTIST?

Hustler or Egghead? Huggy Bear or Einstein? Which best describes YOU? Are you fluent in Technobabble or Jive ass? Do your bitches turn tricks on the street or do they smoke cigarettes chained up in a laboratory? Do you spend your day at the controls of a cyclotron or a Cadillac? Only by answering the questions with HONESTY will you discover the TRUTH.

THE LINE THAT CANNOT LIE

Do you swank down the street like one of the Wooden Tops, acknowledging petty criminals in your wake?

Do you bumble down the street dropping sheets of paper, mumbling and forgetting who you are?

Do you wear big chrome sun-glasses with holes in the arms, even at night?

Have you ever pushed a woman up against a wall and taken a roll of dollar bills out of her bra?

Do you employ upwards of twenty women?

Do you have several biros and a spatula in your pocket?

Do any of them wear lab coats?

Do you have several high ranking police officers in your pocket?

Do you spend some of your time weighing out powders in a laboratory?

Have you ever split the atom?

Do you spend some of your time weighing out powders in a lavatory?

Have you ever been funded by a Government grant?

Have you ever been funded by Hugh Grant?

Do you wear small wire rimmed glasses on top of your head and spend most of the day looking for them?

Is the brim of your hat more than four foot across?

Could you assemble Kipp's apparatus for the production of hydrogen sulphide?

Does your brain weigh more than 4 pounds?

Have you ever looked down a gun-barrel as someone tried to muscle in on your action?

Have you ever split the scene when the going got too hot?

Do you ever put your arms into the sleeves of your coat?

Have you ever removed the top of a monkey's head with a scalpel?

Does your jewellery weigh more than you do?

Have you ever looked down a microscope to study the action of a muscle?

Do you think that the speed of light is absolute and indeed the only universal constant?

Do you think the city is bone dry and that something big is going down?

Did you ever shag Marilyn Monroe?

Have you ever been hit on the back of the head with a pool cue?

Have you ever been shot by David Soul dressed as a motorcycle cop?

Is your car 40 feet long, pink and furry inside?

Do you prefer 'waccy waccy' funk guitar to Bavarian oompah music?

Congratulations! You are a true scientist. You think nothing of locking yourself in a laboratory for weeks on end in your relentless search for knowledge. You are absent minded, loveable and probably bald on top. However, you have a darker side to your nature, a side that wants to meddle in things you don't understand. Tampering with the very fabric of life itself could be your downfall, so beware.

What it is, bro! You're a pimp my man! You're the most baddest arsed motherfucker in the hood. With your cool dude attitude, a car as big as a tennis court and more bitches than Crufts, you strut down the street like a peacock, cutting the meanest silhouette on the Lower East Side. But watch your back. You think you're in charge but some of your ladies may be holding out on you.

Letterbocks

Bum note

❏ I doubt whether John Lennon could have sung the immortal line "What-ever gets you through the night, s'alright, s'alright" with much conviction had he just woken to find his partner anally masturbating with his toothbrush in the early hours.

**Andrew France
Manchester**

❏ I played the latest Beatles single "Free As A Bird" to my pet budgerigar, but he failed totally to see the irony of the situation.

**A. Faith
West Bromwich**

❏ My Grandad always warned us against keeping two pencils in the same pocket. "They could rub together while you're running for a bus, and set your trousers on fire", he'd say. He passed away some years ago, but it is doubtless thanks to him that I have never kept two pencils in the same pocket, and my trousers have never caught fire while running for a bus.

**G. Dog
Kennel, Herts.**

That's Wife

❏ Desmond Wilcox has received a lot of sympathy after announcing that he is going deaf. Frankly, if I was married to Esther Rantzen and found I could no longer hear her voice, I'd need plastic surgery to get the fucking smile off my face.

**G. Fish
Bowl, near Glossop**

❏ I recently visited a small village in Tongo where I sampled the local narcotic brew Kava, made from roots and tasting like grass clippings flavoured pond water. As you can see from the photo, the village was somewhat appropriately named.

**Terry Collister
NSW, Australia**

❏ I'm sick to fuck of newspaper buying bastards who skip the queue just because they've got the right money and they've got a train or bus to catch. Fuck off. If you want to buy a paper, get up earlier, and join the queue like everyone else.

**G. McKendrick
Glasgow**

Open question

❏ If 'open all hours' convenience stores are indeed open 24 hours a day, 365 days a year, why do they have locks on their doors?

**Chad Berscheld
The Internet**

❏ Mustard gas is no substitute for the real thing, especially in ham sandwiches.

**A. K.
Walsall**

❏ Here's an idea for the BBC. How about a new series of Doctor Who. "Doctor Who and the Zero Tolerance Committees". As you can see from this picture of our local group, these feminist monsters would soon have us all hiding behind our settees.

**J.D.
Manchester**

❏ Have any other readers noticed the remarkable resemblance between the recently returned Viz cartoon character Paul Whicker the tall vicar, and Aston Villa's footballing import Sasa Curcic? I wonder if they are perhaps both thin, with pointy tufts of hair and big noses?

**Phil Rainey
Kings Heath, Birmingham**

❏ No such thing as a free lunch? Cobblers. I had a very agreeable meal the other day in a cozy, country pub. It was only after leaving, via the toilet window, that it occurred to me I had completely forgotten to pay the bill.

**P. Koffendrop
Buckfast**

❏ Carly Simon is on record as saying she will not name the subject of her cutting seventies ballad 'You're So Vain' until after his death. Well, that rules Lesley Crowther out then.

**D. Kennel
Arbroath**

2p or not 2p

❏ Poor people shouldn't worry too much if they don't have two pennies to rub together. I tried it the other day, and frankly can't see what all the fuss is about.

**S. Hope
Long Eaton**

❏ We hear so much about the upset caused by people receiving poison pen letters nowadays. Isn't it about time the Government banned the sale of all poison pens?

**F. Tank
Sideboard, Lancs.**

I guess that's why they call him a cunt

❑ I parked my van on a meter in Kensington one day and Elton John pulls up in his Bentley and tells me to move it so that he can park there. Cheeky shoe bonkers rug headed cunt.

M. Warren
Crowthorne, Berks.

❑ In 1983 I was walking out of Victoria station when I spotted sixties chirpy cockney character Jo Brown, of guitar strumming and children's road safety fame. I gave him a friendly nod, and he acknowledged this with a smile and a nod of his own. All was well and good between us until July of last year when I was working in a motorway service station on the M42. One night who should walk in but my old mate Jo. He stayed for 15 minutes, during which time the miserable fucker pretended not to recognise me.
I had the last laugh though, because his bird was definitely giving me the eye when she asked where the toilets were.

M. Barber
Newcastle-under-Lyme

❑ That Tommy Cannon opened a fair near us once, and even though he was getting paid he stood throughout the entire day with a face like a kicked in fridge door. The sour faced bastard.

Andy Reynolds
Selby, North Yorks.

* This is a cunts competition, Andy. Bastards - sour faced or otherwise - don't qualify.

Brief encunter

❑ My brother Dave is a postman in Devon and was awaiting a delivery of mail at Newton Abbott station when Danny La Rue swanned up to him and ordered him to shift two cases of girlie dresses across the bridge to the other platform. When Dave explained he was a postman rather than a porter, the cross-dressing cunt called my brother a "lazy bastard" and ponced off with his nose in the air.

Tom R.
Northampton

Plucking cunt

❑ Throughout my teens I was an ardent fan of the Who's brilliant rock guitarist Pete Townsend. I even bought his solo LP 'Who Came First' in 1973. Then one magical day whilst visiting London I saw my hero Pete Townsend striding along Oxford Street, heading straight towards me.
God! My heart was in my mouth, my legs turned to jelly as I sidled up to him with a hopeful, admiring smile on my face. And yes! He actually spoke to me. "Get out of my fucking way" he said.

J. Truscott
Plymouth

He is not a number. He is a cunt.

❑ At the 1996 cult TV convention dedicated to 60s TV series The Prisoner, actor and guest speaker Alexis Kanner waved off an excited fan who'd requested his autograph by turning his back on him and saying "Try again tomorrow". The ginger haired cunt.

Tee
Brondesbury Park
London

Do ya think I'm cunty?

❑ About six years ago I saw that tartan twat Rod "He's foot-ball crazy" Stewart and his blonde tart shopping at Safeways in Henley. I'm a big fan of his grating voice and ugly features, so I politely asked him to sign my till receipt.
"I don't sign scraps of paper" he said. Croaky cunt.

Mark Griffiths
Nomura International
London

You're a lady He's a cunt

❑ At a theatre where I worked I was asked to prepare a sandwich for singer Peter Skellern, and the cunt turned his nose up at it. Twenty years later I'm still making sandwiches. Where is Peter Skellern nowadays, eh?

R. Ingram
Leicester

❑ I detect a slight bias against women in your organ. Why use words like cunt and twat to describe men? What about prick, or dickhead, etc. etc. Come on. Fair's fair.

A grandmother of three
Lewisham

* Daft bint.

❑ I used to work at a 24 hour petrol station outside Bristol and there were times when I had to fight the celebrity cunts off with a stick. Jim Davidson

threatened to fill my face in one evening, Chris Searle off That's Life told me to "fuck off" simply because I said "Thank you, Mr Searle". And Pete Willis out of Def Leppard, who was pissed at the time, got shirty when I told him his Access card had expired.
But they weren't all cunts. Tony 'Baldrick' Robinson was a regular customer and he was a really nice guy and a joy to flog petrol to.

Jon Wisbey
Brislington, Bristol

You see that cunt? That's YOU that is

❑ I was working as a waitress in a hotel in Norwich (as opposed to a cocktail bar) when so-called comedian Rob Newman, who'd played a gig in town the night before, came down for breakfast. He was too late for a full English breakfast but I went out of my way to get him a bowl of scrambled egg. While I was preparing this the rotten bastard stole the mushrooms and bacon from my own breakfast plate which was keeping warm on a heated sideboard in the dining room. This breakfast was the only perk I got from my shitty paid job, and something that kept me going from 5.30am when I started until late morning when lazy, thieving, long hairs like Newman crawl out of bed and muster themselves 'together man' with numerous pots of tea and coffee that frankly I wish I'd pissed in.
In fact, if he's reading this, I did piss in it. And the chef whacked off in your scrambled eggs too.

Miss S.E.Hall
Jesmond, Newcastle

❑ I took my bird for a dirty weekend in Lowestoft and we met Emlyn Hughes and Willy Thorne. Surprisingly Willie Thorne, who looks like a cunt, turned out to be a twat and Emlyn Hughes, who looks like a tosser, was just a bell-end.

Simon Nielson
Wirral, Merseyside

DOCTOR. I CAN'T GET AN ERECTION.

FILL UP with brussel sprouts at lunchtime on Christmas Day, then go carol singing in the afternoon. Try and contain your obnoxious farts until the pause immediately after "five gold rings" for maximum comic effect.

Run Rig
Loch Lomond

POUR a handful of tiny ball bearings into your socks each morning to make them easier to remove come the evening.

Paul Atkin
Ipswich

AT £300 a Psion personal organiser makes the ideal Christmas gift for someone who wants to know whether its batteries are running out yet.

P. A.
Suffolk

ELIMINATE irritating shadows next time you go outside by shining a powerful torch at them.

P.A.
Ipswich

LARD ARSES. Enjoy a healthier fried breakfast by sprinkling washing powder with fat digesters onto it instead of salt.

N. Opee
Kew

PET shop owners. When planning your shop layout, position slow moving animals like tortoises near the exits to give them a better chance of escape in the event of a fire.

S.R.
Grimsby

PLASTIC UHT cream and milk cartons from service stations make ideal 'Quaker hats' for Action Men.

M.F. Phillips
Burton-upon-Trent

AIR HOSTESSES. Make pulling your trolley easier by asking aisle passengers to dip their elbows in a saucer of lubricating oil before take off.

John Kean
Docklands

BORED housewives. Make your hubby look like James Bond by looking at him through an old toilet roll tube.

John Tait
Thropton

FATTIES. Put a banana in each side of your mouth then look in a mirror. Elephant features.

A. Bottlebank (green only)
Asda Carpark

JACK Charlton. Give your brother Bobby a Shredded Wheat for Christmas. Cut in half and glued to his baldy scalp it will resemble an attractive head of hair with a neat centre parting.

Martin Emmerson
Hartlepool

AVOID paying over the odds for hardback books. Simply buy the paperback version, immerse it in water, then pop it into the freezer for 3 hours.

A.S.
Edinburgh

WRITE down the price of everything you buy so that in years to come you can annoy your grandchildren with greater accuracy.

M. Traintu
Georgia

CREATE the effect of 'weightlessness' in your own home by carrying your wife (or husband) around on your shoulders all day. After tea, put them down. For a few seconds you will have the same feeling of weightlessness, or 'micro gravity', experienced by astronauts in space.

Sue Wester
Gloucester

FARMERS. Treat your sheep to a Marks and Spencers party dip this year. Cucumber and yoghurt, blue cheese, or perhaps even oriental herbs and spices flavour. They'll make a lovely change from sheep dip, and have the advantage of containing no organo phosphates.

U. D.
Marsworth, Bucks.

TAKE your own cheese slice to McDonalds. Pop it into a hamburger and hey presto! A cheeseburger. This money saving tip was brought to you buy Tim Wilkes.

T. Wilkes
Groundhurst, Kent

RICE pudding eaters. Take a tip from pond owners. Place a ping pong ball on top of your pudding. When a skin forms, simply remove the ball leaving a neat hole through which to eat the pudding.

J.T.
Imblingham

GARDENERS. As the winter draws in, remove the fingers from old woollen gloves to make handy frost covers for your carrots.

J. Tait
Thropton

FILL a flat fish with hot butter last thing at night and it makes an ideal hot water bottle. Wake up in the morning and 'voila!' A ready cooked kipper for breakfast in bed.

Barry Clarver
Exeter

BREAST feeding mothers. Pop a fresh tea bag into each bra cup. They'll absorb any excess milk, avoiding embarrassing stains. Later you can drop them into a cup of boiling water to make sweet, ready milked tea.

Urinal Dockrat
Marsworth, Bucks.

A HEDGEHOG trained to scuttle up and down the table from guest to guest makes an unusual mobile cheese and pineapple cube nibble dispenser at cocktail parties.

L. Traintu
Clarkesville

CAN'T afford a colour telly? Simply smear your black and white telly screen with Grecian 2000. Hey presto! Your picture will gradually turn to colour. Possibly.

Martin Harwood
Marketing Director
Grecian 2000 (UK) Ltd,
Bradford

CONVINCE neighbours that you have invented a 'shrinking' device by ruffling your hair, wearing a white laboratory coat, and parking a JCB digger outside your house for a few days. Then dim and flicker the lights in your house during the night and replace the JCB, unseen, with a Tonka toy of the same description. Watch their faces the next morning!

Prof. J. Francis
Rhondda

CARRY on looking for lost items for a few moments after you have found them. That way they will not "always be in the last place you look".

Luke Tucker
Hayes, Middlesex

COAT exterior doors with strawberry jam. It has an attractive textured, glossy effect, but its principal advantage over traditional wood finishes is that it traps flies, which can then be swatted at your convenience.

R. R.
Nottingham

CONVERT trainers to temporary football boots by melting the base of Rolos and gently sticking them to the sole.

Eric Twilley
Reading

FOR an extra long Christmas kiss swap your girlfriend's Lipsyl for a Prittstick.

Mr Bond
Eyepresume

ORANGE peel makes an ideal substitute for dried apricot, and tastes pretty much the same.

J.T.
Northumberland

EVADE hose pipe bans by painting your garden hose pink and threading it up your trouser leg and out of your flies.

S. D. T.
Hexham

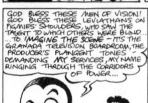

SPOILT BASTARD's CHRISTMAS CAROL

XMAS EVE... THUNK!

QUICKER, WOMAN. **QUICKER!** YOU'RE NEVER GOING TO EARN ENOUGH TO BUY ME A BIKE FOR CHRISTMAS AT THIS RATE. YOU'LL HAVE TO SPEED UP IF YOU'RE GOING TO EARN THAT LAST £5 BEFORE MORNING...

...AND DON'T FORGET, THE BICYCLE SHOP MAN IS OPENING UP ESPECIALLY FOR YOU AT EIGHT O'CLOCK

OH, TIMMY... **PLEASE** LET ME REST MY HEAD ON THE TABLE, JUST FOR A MINUTE... I'VE BEEN UP SINCE MARCH

DON'T BE SO **SELFISH!** NOW I'M OFF TO BED. I DON'T WANT TO MISS SANTA. I'LL BE DOWN AT EIGHT THIRTY, AND IF HE HASN'T BROUGHT ME A BIKE, I'LL NEVER FORGIVE YOU... ...**EVER!**

K-CLICK!

SHORTLY... OH, LORD... LOOK AT THE TIME... K-CLICK

4.00 a.m... YAAAWN!! I'LL JUST CLOSE MY EYES FOR TWO MINUTES... ...I'LL NOT FALL ASLEEP... THUNK!

...JUST TWO MINUTES... ...NOT...FALL...ASLEEP. ......SO....T...TIRED... NOT...FALL...ASLEEP... **NO!**..NOT FALL...FALL...

SNORE! SNORE! SNORE!

WOOOOOOO EH!?!..WHASSAT!?! OH, GOD...**NO!**.. I'VE BEEN ASLEEP!

WOOoooOOOooooO! I AM THE GHOST OF CHRISTMAS MRS. TIMPSON. I'VE COME TO SHOW YOU WHAT WILL HAPPEN TO TIMMY IF YOU DON'T GET HIM A BIKE...

BUT LET'S START AT THE BEGINNING A CHRISTMAS PAST... DO YOU REMEMBER FIVE YEARS AGO IN THAT COSY LITTLE HOUSE?

...DO YOU RECOGNISE ANYONE, MRS. TIMPSON? YES...**YES!** I DO! ...IT'S ME AND MY HUSBAND AND LITTLE BABY TIMMY!

THERE YOU ARE, TIMMY...A NICE NEW RATTLE. I HOPE YOU LIKE IT. HAPPY FIRST CHRISTMAS, MY DARLING... ...SNIFF! RATTLE! RATTLE!

CRACK!

ME DON'T WANT THAT **SHIT!** ME WANT TRACEY ISLAND. ME SEE IT ON TELLY. IT THIRTY NINE NINETY NINE. GOO-GOO-BITCH

THAT'S IT, CISSY. I'VE SEEN ALL I NEED TO...**I'M OFF!** GOOD LUCK!

SOB! SOB! OH, TIMMY, I'M SO..SO... SORRY... SOB!! I'VE RUINED YOUR FIRST CHRISTMAS...SOB! SOB! SOB! YES!

OH HE WAS A LOVELY BABY...A VERY STRONG PERSONALITY... AND HE THOUGHT THE WORLD OF ME COME WITH ME TO CHRISTMAS PRESENT NOW, MRS. TIMPSON

OH, MUMMY...A BEAUTIFUL SHINEY RED BICYCLE.... ...THANK YOU...THANK YOU!!

OH, I LOVE YOU SO MUCH, MUMMY... I WANT TO HUG YOU FOREVER AND GIVE YOU A MILLION KISSES! I'M FILLING UP...SNIFF!

IT'S THE NICEST AND MOST EXPEN- SIVE PRESENT YOU'VE EVER BOUGHT ME

OH, ISN'T THAT LOVELY!?! YES. BUT LET US LOOK AT CHRISTMAS YET TO COME AND SEE WHAT WILL BE IF YOU DON'T BUY HIM THE BICYCLE

TIMMY, THAT WAS JOHNNY ON THE PHONE. HE SAID DO YOU WANT TO GO ROUND TO HIS HOUSE AND PLAY WITH HIS BICYCLE? SHUFFLE! SHUFFLE!

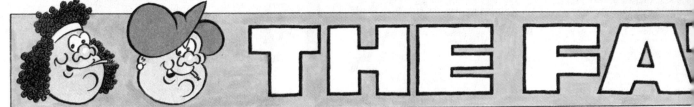

SLAGS

ANYWAY, I DON'T KNOW WHAT Y'RUSH IS. NOBODY'S GOIN' T' FUCK **YOU** TONIGHT... YER ON YER RAGS!

SO? I'VE GOT A GOB, AIN'T I?

RITZY'S NIGHTCLUB PLEASE, SPIROS

RIGHTY-HO, MATEY PEEPS... BIG LADIES JIGGY JIGGY TONIGHT, EH?

NOT 'ER... SHE'S GOT THE PAINTERS IN

H...! STAYIN' ALIVE... STAYIN'...! AAAH! STAYIN' AL-II-EE-AAA..."

JAB! JAB! JAB!

AYUP THERE, BAZ. CAN WE JOIN YER?

OH AYUP, GIRLS... AYE, COURSE Y'CAN

HEY... D'Y'FANCY A DRINK, BAZ?

AYE... I'D **LOVE** ONE

OH, YEH?

WELL GOIN' T' HAVE OK **ME** FIRST...

THEM'S **MY** BIRDS, Y'TWO BOB FART. I KNOW **YOUR** SORT... 'ARD AS NAILS AN' JUST AS EASY TO FUCKIN' 'AMMER. C'MON THEN, IF Y'THINK Y'BIG ENOUGH...Y' DON'T FUCKIN' SCARE **ME**. Y' DON'T THE BIGGER THEY ARE THE 'ARDER THEY...

WAM!

FALL...

OOH, LOOK, TRAY... THEY'RE FIGHTIN' OVER US

AYE... I'NT IT ROMANTIC

... EEH, BAZ...YORRA FUCKIN' 'ERO!

AYE... COMIN' T' THE RESCUE O' TWO DAMSONS IN DISTRESS

Y'VE WON US 'ANDS, BAZ

AYE... AN' US FANNIES. LET'S GO 'OME AN' WE'LL GIVE YOU A PROPER SEEIN' TO

GROAN!

SO...

CHOKE!... AAAH... 'OSPITAL!

IS 'E UP FORRIT YET, TRAYZ?

NAH! MIND YOU, 'E DID LOSE A LOT OF BLOOD ON THE WAY 'OME. I'LL GIVE 'IM ANOTHER TEN MINUTES

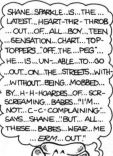

Conditions were not condusive to open, attractive football and both teams stuggled to string fluid attacking moves together.

It was a day for the long ball, with both teams playing the percentage game.

OOOF!

But with mud up to three feet deep in places, attempts on goal were few and far between.

After a dissappointing ninety minutes the game remained goal-less, when suddenly...

PHEEEP!

Penalty to England!

England were one spot kick away from the greatest football victory in the history of World War One. It would take a brave man indeed to step forward and take this, the most important penalty kick in history.

Come on then, lads. We need a volunteer

No thanks!

Sorry mate. Not likely.

Rather you than me

One by one Tommy's team mates shunned the challenge.

In the absence of volunteers, Tommy bravely stepped forward to take the kick himself...

My god! If he misses, it will haunt him for the rest of his life.

...but as he ran towards the spot, the luckless Tommy stood on a land mine.

AAAARGH!

BOOM!

When the dust settled...

It's your crucient ligament, Tommy. It's gone completely. You'll be out for six to eight weeks.

Someone else will have to take the penalty.

No. Tommy had started to take the penalty , so only he can finish it.

But...

Don't worry, sir. I can do it!

All eyes were on Tommy as once again he prepared to take the kick.

Good luck, Tommy. God be with you.

You heff to admire ze Englander's spunk.

BOOT!

Hooray! Hooray for Tommy!

Did I score? Did it go in.

Yes, Tommy. A perfect spot kick.

I'll remember this day for the rest of my life!

Of the winning England eleven, only Tommy Typhoon survived to tell the tale. For under strict military law his ten team mates who had shirked the responsibility of taking the vital spot kick were - quite rightly - court martialed for cowardice in the face of the enemy. They were shot on Boxing Day 1917, and buried in an unmarked grave.

Blind, and with only one leg, Tommy Typhoon was sent home to spend the rest of the war in the care of his family. Sadly he was arrested at Dover by military police and shot as a deserter due to an administrative hiccup.

To this day his grave, in the shadow of Accrington Accademicals football ground, is a shrine for fans of football and World War One alike.

The end

124

TOP OF THE BOTS!

Sexy secrets of sizzling
TV stunner Sam's arse

IT'S no coincidence that sexy Samantha Janus's name rhymes with anus. For that's exactly what the sizzling telly stunner has got.

At the bottom of her back Sam boasts two buttocks. And those, together with the hole in between, are her arse. And its an arse which is rapidly becoming Sam's prized *asset*. For as well as turning the fella's heads, Sam's raunchy rear doubles as a cute cushion for her to sit on.

PILLOW

"My arse is soft - just like a pillow. So when I sit on it, my bones don't hurt", the stunning TV sexpot told us yesterday. But fellas hoping to inspect Sam's sumptuous behind at close quarters should beware. For it has a third, slightly less saucy, function. After Sam has ate something, shit comes out of it.

SMALL

Sam's ca-*rear* took off after she was chosen to represent Britain in the Eurovision Song Contest. Sadly she didn't *winnit*, but it wasn't long after that her shapely turd hopper began to catch the eye and TV roles quickly followed.

CARELESS

Wherever Sam goes her bum - which is pink and made out of skin - is never far behind. Even when she's filming her hit TV comedy series 'Pie In The Sky'. But the last thing the TV temptress wants is a pie in her pants. So she regularly visits the toilet to empty her bowel. And to avoid being nominated for the Eurovision *Pong* Contest, stunner Sam makes sure her shute is well wiped before she leaves the ladies.

RECKLESS

"Fellas can't get enough of my ring", sexpot Sam revealed after her arse was voted Britain's Best Butt by readers of *Swelling Bollocks* maga-zine. Indeed, her panty peach is so popular she permanently keeps it under wraps. Trousers, knickers and skirts make up an impressive arsenal of protective clothing, keeping the star's bot hot in winter, and well away from prying eyes.

PLASTIC

Sam's Italian boyfriend, former stripper Mauro Manero, is probably her arse's number one fan. "But even he gives my jacksie a wide birth when I've got one in the bomb bay", says the bubbly beauty who once appeared in a TV ad for fish fingers.

JILTED

Having a plum bum means that sexy Sam is spoilt for choice when it comes to farting. For the petite songstress can fart out of either of two holes - her arse or her chuff.

Nice arse, eh fellas? Stunning Sam's raunchy rear view.

Bot's it all about?

LIKE so many of the stars, Sam shrouds her arse in secrecy. But we decided to get to the *bottom* of it by revealing ten things you never knew about her beautiful blowhole.

1. Sam's arse muscle - the sphincter - works the opposite way round to a tube of tooth-paste. Unlike most muscles which contract only when in use, Sam's sphincter permanently pulls - or contracts - in order to keep her bum shut. When she feels the turtle's head, Sam moves her bowel by deliberately relaxing the muscle whilst sitting on the toilet.

2. Sam's bum helps keep her trousers up by being wider than her waist, which is directly above it.

4. Just like teeth, arses can fall out too. A 'fuil rectal pro-lapse' is what doctors would call it if Sam's arse literally fell out!

5. Piles are Sam's arse's worst enemy. They is what its called when blood vessels up the bum get big and fat and start to look like David Pleat's haircut.

Nowadays doctors can remove them in seconds using red hot metal scissors.

9. Sam's bumcheeks - the two *sides* of her arse - go up and down alternately when she is walking. This undulation takes place in a vertical plane, and is symetrically inverted along the axis of her bum crack. Scientists call this aesthetically appealing phenomm-mmm....mmmmmmom... a "wiggle".

10. Sam's arse is one of nature's minia-ture perfume factories. Natural odours are emit-ted from Sam's bot, despite her best efforts to prevent them. Many of these smells are so slight that the human nose cannot detect them. But if Sam were to walk around a council estate with no pants on, on a very hot day, packs of dogs would probably chase her, and frantically sniff her arse.

Your views on SAM'S ANUS

WE took to the streets to ask some of Britain's fellas what they thought about Samantha's sizzling bumhole.

BRICKLAYER **Kevin Cresswell** specu-lated that Sam's bottom would be much easier to wipe than his own.
He, 34, said "I've got a great big fat arse, and it can be a nightmare cleaning up after a few beers and a curry. I'd imagine Sam's is much easier to look after than my own".

QUANTITY SURVEYOR **Ian Hall**, 42, admits he is puzzled by the workings of Sam's sphincter. The dad of two, from Malton, North Yorks, said "If Sam has to constantly contract her sphincter muscle in order to keep her stools at bay, as it says elsewhere on this page, then how come she doesn't shit herself every time she goes to sleep?"

ZOOLOGIST **Trevor Gregory**, 18, who works at a zoo in Salford, Manchester, said that if Sam was a monkey, and was modelling for page three of a monkey tabloid, she would have to bare her bottom, not her breasts.
"Men monkeys don't go much on tits. They prefer ogling the lady monkeys' backsides. So did humans, when we were monkeys, many years ago. Nowadays we've stood up, and turned into people. We like tits most of all. But monkeys still prefer arses."

No doubt there's a few cheeky monkeys out there reading this who wouldn't mind getting their hands on Sam's arse! Or perhaps sticking a banana up it.

The MODERN PARENTS

"Can we have ten pounds?"

"I'm not sure, Tarquin... what's it for?"

"I want to take Guin to see... er... an *interactive performance art experience* which... er... introduces young people to elements of Northern European folk lore and mythology."

"Gosh! That sounds interesting! Where's it on?"

"'S at Shopping City... we're going to see Santa!"

"Guin! Shhh!"

"Oh Tarquin! You were planning to go to that *awful* Santa's Palace experience, weren't you?"

"But it's really good! They've got these jet-sleighs which you ride around this track, with special effects and moving animals and everything!"

"'S wicked!"

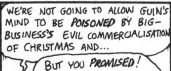

"We're not going to allow Guin's mind to be *poisoned* by big-business's evil commercialisation of Christmas and..."

"But you *promised*! You promised if me and Guin came back from our Greek island* we could have a *proper* Christmas this year!"

*See Issue 78

"We *are* going to have a *proper* Christmas... don't forget, Malcolm and I are taking you to the Winter Solstice Craft-Fayre at the weekend..."

"Oh yes!.. that! We can't *wait*, can we, Guin?"

"Want to see Santa."

"Don't worry.... you've just given me an idea! Cressida and I will organise a special surprise for you and Guin and all the other young people, after the Fayre..."

ETHICALLY AWARE PARENTS' COMMITTEE
Winter Solstice Craft Fayre

"Eight quid! For a candle! If this isn't commercialization, I don't know what is!"

"Don't be *silly*, Tarquin! These are hand-made objects made by crafts persons who work for the love of it."

Non-phallic Candles — £8

HOMELESS

Modern Nativity Refugee Crib Figures. £80 a set

"Oh look, Herbie, we must get one of these tree stumps for our mulled grape-juice and sugar-free mince pie party"

Anti-deforestation Xmas Tree Stumps £90

SAVE THE FORESTS   FELLED FOR GREED   CONIFERS HAVE RIGHTS

Recycled Junk Trees £20

"..and you wrote all these yourselves? They're so *clever*! Listen to this one, Amy! "Good King Wenceslas looked out, Early in the morning, There wasn't any snow about Because of global warming." HA HA!"

CARING CAROLS New lyrics for a New Age Bob & Zoe Green

"I'm bored."

"So am I."

"You won't be in a minute... gather Guinevere and all the other toddlers together, Tarquin, and bring them through to the other hall in five minutes..."

THE FATHER CHRISTMAS EXPERIENCE

"HMM..."

"Hello, boys and girls!"

"It's your dad, Amy..."

"Come on, everybody! Into the sledges! We're going to see Father Christmas!"

"Oh well, I suppose at least they're trying..."

"Hi! I'm Pasha the Polar Bear! I'm a peace-loving, non-aggressive animal, living at the North Pole, at one with nature... come with me to the home of Father Christmas..."

"Look, reindeer!"

"Come on, everybody, join in our *reindeer dance*... move with *flowing, willowy* movements...."

"When do we get our presents?"

"And look! It's Father Christmas!"

"Ho ho ho!"

"Why are you laughing, Santa?"